STILL SINGING
Ancora Cantando

Michele (Mike) Costantini

Copyright © 2021, Michele Costantini

All rights reserved.

Except for brief excerpts for review purposes, no part of this book may be reproduced or used in any form without written permission from the publisher.

ISBN 978-0-6451823-2-3

BIOGRAPHY & AUTOBIOGRAPHY/Cultural, Ethnic & Regional/General

Michele (Mike) Costantini began life in the beautiful town of Ari, in the Abruzzi region of central Italy. His idyllic, young lifestyle was shattered with the death of his young mother, and then the assault of World War II. Following the war, destiny led Mike to immigrate to Australia, where he gratefully grasped every opportunity, working hard to build a new life. He met his Australian wife Betty and together they raised a family on their farm north of Brisbane. From his boyhood Italian feste to writing his own songs and recording a CD in Australia when he was 93 years old, Mike has always loved music. He wrote his biography, 'Still Singing' Ancora Cantando, when he was 94 years old.

Singing at one of my grandchildren's weddings

My family is everything to me, so this book is for my family.

CONTENTS

INTRODUCTION	1
ABOUT ME - MICHELE	3
MY FAMILY AND I	6
MY EARLY DAYS	25
WORLD WAR II AND THE END OF LIFE AS WE KNEW IT	38
RE-BUILDING OUR LIVES AFTER THE WAR	75
BECOMING A MAN	97
BECOMING NATIONALISED AND BUILDING THE FARM	158
FAMILY LIFE	185
IL FINALE (OF MY BOOK - NOT ME!)	196
MY SONGS	198

INTRODUCTION

My book is a recollection of my life's experiences, including as a migrant's journey, having been born in Italy and lived most of my life in Australia.

It is for me to reach back and remember so I might share my journey with my family, so they might understand our heritage. It is for friends I have met along the way and for anyone interested in my story.

It recalls my childhood, growing up in the beautiful town of Ari, Chieti province, in the Abruzzi region of central Italy. It moves through darker times in Europe and World War II and brutal events that changed the history of the world and the future of my lineage.

My recollections touch on my life as a young migrant in Australia, including taking jobs over much of the country in search of opportunity, along with milestones like meeting my wife Betty, raising a family, enjoying sports, running a business, and writing and recording songs.

I have always enjoyed music. First in our village feste in Italy, then studying music later in Australia, learning the 'fisarmonica' (piano-accordion), taking singing lessons, singing songs I have written and recorded, and others that I enjoy.

Events in my story are spread across four continents (Italy, South America, North America, Australia), over three centuries and four generations. Stories are retold that I learnt from my parents, about their lives and history.

I wrote my story in my native Italian language and my children have helped me translate my book from Italian to English. They have researched and included some of the historical facts surrounding my life's experiences.

ABOUT ME - MICHELE

I have done many things in my life, but most of my time has been living and working on farms, first in Italy and then Australia. That's been by choice mostly and I am very happy being outside in the sun, growing and raising healthy plants and trees, able to pick fresh fruit straight from nature.

It's a paradise here on our four-hectare farm, and I feel lucky to be able to go to my garden every day in the mornings and afternoons. Today, I just put six posts in and some trellises for my passionfruit. They are amazingly sweet this year!

At the time of writing my book, I am 94 years old and live with my wife Betty on our farm. I work outside every day in the garden, enjoy healthy food and a glass of wine. Until recently, I made my own wine using the old methods from Italy. I still sing every day, in my studio, in the shower and in the garden.

Anyone who knows me, knows that I enjoy sharing my stories, which is what this book is all about.

The war that changed everything

My early life was an incredible time to be alive. The little village where I was born, Ari, and our province of Abruzzo, were a paradise of rich agricultural soils, old village traditions and beautifully spirited people.

Remote rural Italians like us, living between the Apennine Mountains and the Adriatic Sea on Italy's east coast, enjoyed a simple life before the war. We worked hard on the land, and spent time with friends and family, as much as we could, and this was the most important thing.

I was 12 when World War II started in 1939, and the formative years of my youth coincided with some of the darkest moments in Italy's history.

At the outset of the war, the course that this brutal event would take and its full impact on our lives, was unknown to us. It impoverished Europe and shaped our lives forevermore, bringing me and so many others from one side of the world to the other.

There can be no way to overstate the impact the war had on our village as the Front swept right through our province.

Nazis evicted us from our homes and the Allies carpet-bombed the countryside.

Caught in the crossfire, we lived our lives looking for signs of hope that a time would come to replace what had become our daily battle to survive. Refugees in our own country, our hearts did not once stop hoping to return to the simple but free life we once enjoyed.

That hope was finally rewarded when Germany surrendered in May 1945. The dreadful war was finally over. With Italy liberated by the Allied and (by then) Italian forces, the monumental task of rebuilding our lives and re-establishing our farming lifestyles lay ahead of us. The fighting was over, but our lives would never be the same again.

Italy did eventually re-prosper as a nation decades later, though I was not there to see that, having by then made a new life on the other side of the world. Would I have ever gone to Australia without having lived through the war? Who can tell? I can say that I have never stopped considering myself fortunate for having had the opportunity and the gift of making Australia my home.

MY FAMILY AND I

Where to start when writing about 94 years of one's history? Family is everything to Italians, so I begin with an introduction to my family, past and present, in Australia and overseas, to set the scene for the stories to come.

By way of introduction, I came from Italy to Australia in 1952 and have my immediate family here, including my wife Betty whom I adore after 64 years of marriage. Our best times are when we are with our family of five children: Tony, Linda, Peter, Diana and Len, our ten grandchildren and growing number of great grandchildren, all very dear to us.

It is a great gift to also have family in Italy, Argentina, North America and Sydney, Australia. We are always one family, connected by our history, despite the distance.

My Grandparents, Michelangelo (Michele) and Antonia Costantini

I was named after my grandfather, but sadly, I never met my grandparents. My father Giustino was the second oldest of their six children. One of his brothers died two months after birth, and his sister died when she was 26 years old. I never met my uncles or aunt on my father's side.

My grandfather owned some small properties in Ari, within 3-4km of each other. I estimate around 4-5 hectares in total. This, he inherited from his father, and his father from his father, and so on. I don't know for how many generations the land was in our family, but we can trace my ancestral family in Ari back many generations to the 1600's.

Sometime after 1904, after the birth of all their children, my grandparents and family left Italy for Argentina. The Argentinian Government promised that large amounts of land could be secured and worked successfully, with good profit. One property in Ari was sold to help pay for sea passage and expenses of buying the land and house in Argentina. Before they left, my grandparents arranged for someone to look after the remaining farms in Italy.

From what my father told me, my grandfather intended to go to Argentina and assess opportunities before deciding whether to remain or return to Italy. My grandparents chose to stay in Argentina, to run their farm and raise their family, and they never returned to Italy.

FAMILY TREE

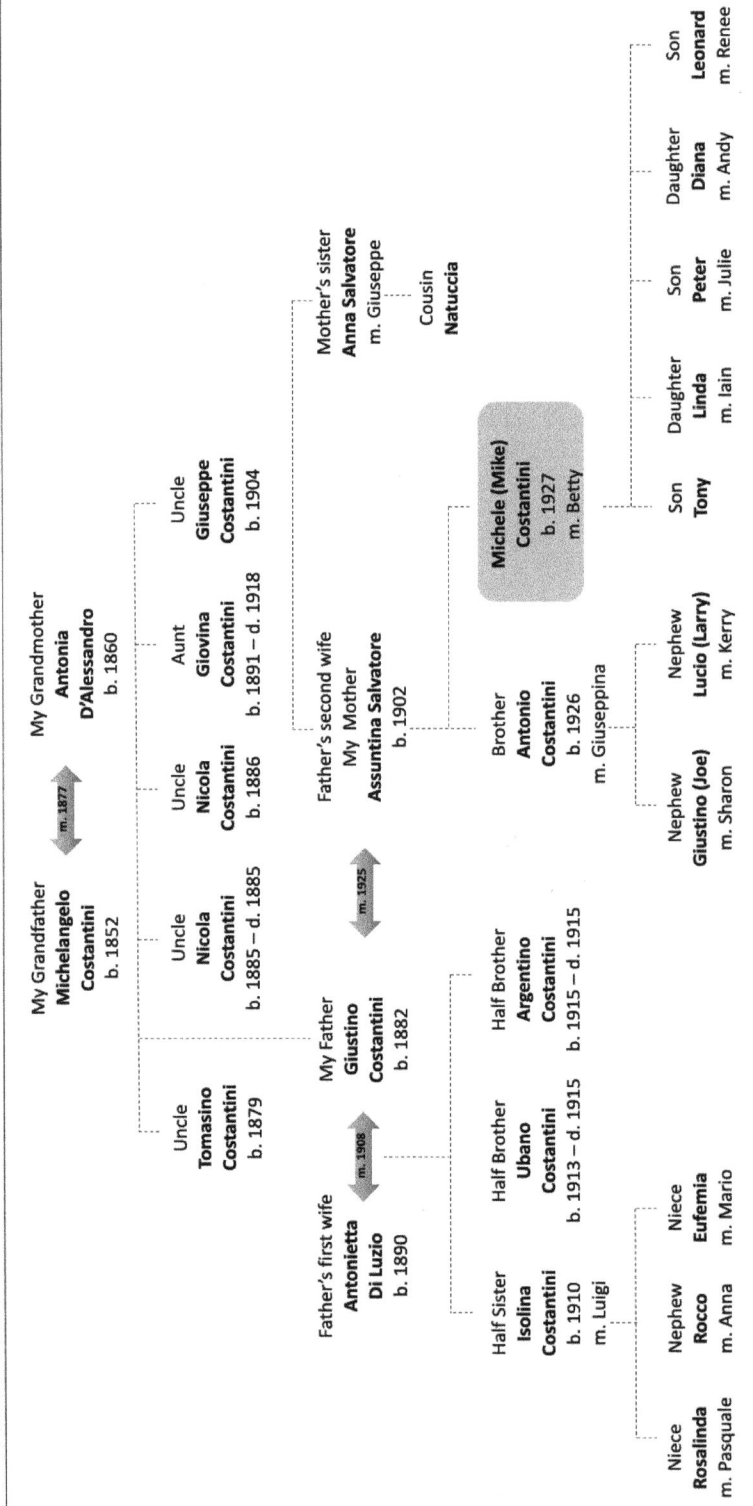

My father was born in his father's house in Ari, in October 1882. He grew to be a big man, with chestnut-coloured eyes. He loved to sing and had a very good voice. Even though he didn't attain a high school education, he would learn to speak three languages - Italian, Spanish and English. This allowed him to work in Argentina and North America and became a lifesaver for some people who we met during the war.

Before my birth, my father lived in Argentina, with his family, on their farm. However due to circumstances that will unfold, he was destined to return to Italy where he inherited both of grandfather's houses, stables, and the land around Ari.

The two Ari houses were close to each other. My father, brother Antonio and I, lived in one, and my cousin Natuccia and her mother Anna, my mother's sister, lived in the other. My father managed both households, running the farms and finances as a single family.

Like mine, his calling was farming, working the fertile Abruzzo land in Italy. There were no tractors in those days. Most work was done by hand, with large animals used for the heavier work. Cows were used to pull ploughs to till soil and donkeys and cows carried loads. Holding and guiding the plough as it was pulled by cows was hard, sometimes requiring long hours. My father, with the family's help, produced food for our table and for sale.

While working in mines in North America, my father contracted a lung condition. We always thought it was bronchitis, but it could have been the black lung disease that many miners contracted because they worked without masks, breathing in coal dust. His lungs never healed properly, and his condition was aggravated during the winter months.

In summer, he worked very hard on the farm. In winter, when he was unwell, he sat in front of our big fireplace, and helped us by working on farm implements. He made handles for chipping hoes, using timber from the nut trees, and canisters or baskets from cane. In winter, we got together with friends and all played cards, gambling with the smallest coins.

I worked with my father and brother on our family farms from age 5 to 24 years old, when I migrated to Australia. I left Italy never dreaming that I would not see my father again. Eight months after I immigrated, in early October 1952, I got the devastating news that the lung disease had killed him. He was only 70 years old.

Bandits on the train

While in Argentina, my father worked with two of his brothers – Nicolo, a senior person in the Buenos Aires railway services, and Giuseppe, who trained young gymnasts. Another brother, Tomasino, had a shop for motorcycle and car parts.

My father worked with Nicolo in the railway services until one fateful day. In the early 20th century, parts of Argentina were still frontier country and bandits roamed the countryside. My father was shocked to discover bandits loading their horses and guns onto a back carriage of the train he worked on. They demanded he keep his mouth shut about them being there and not to tell railway authorities. He refused to keep quiet, and one bandit started a fist fight with him.

My father was not a small man and he fought back with success until another bandit shot him in the leg. Pointing the pistol at his chest, they kicked him off the train. This was in a remote area and my father, losing blood, had no idea how far the next town or doctor were.

Hours later, a man with a horse and carriage came across my father. This Good Samaritan took him to the next town, where his wound was treated. My father stayed there until his leg healed, leaving permanent scarring, and that was the end of his railway career!

The great escape

My father suffered more hardship when he tried to help two teenage boys who worked on his father's farm. The boys were tired of farm work and were keen to find other jobs, so my father travelled with them to Rosario, to help them search for work.

What he didn't know was, in Argentina, in the early 20th century, there was an outbreak of the Bubonic Plague. Tragically, both boys contracted the plague and died. My father was forcibly quarantined by police in Rosario, as part of their efforts to stop the disease spreading. Devastated by the boys' deaths, he lived in fear of contracting the disease. This fear was partly because of primitive conditions in quarantine. There were very little modern facilities or sanitisation. Cutlery was not available. Before he ate, my father plunged his hands into scalding water, as hot as he could bear it, to help protect from infection. Perhaps this and other cautions, helped him avoid contracting the plague.

Convinced that he was not infected, my father believed his best opportunity to survive was to get out of the quarantine area as soon as possible. He had befriended a native South American who did not want to escape himself, but after a lot of convincing, he agreed to help my father.

The quarantine area was enclosed by a wall topped with sharp steel barricades. My father and his friend monitored police movements outside the area, to determine the best time to make a move. With only a few moments to get it right, he stood on his friend's shoulders, and protecting himself with blankets, scaled the barricade to the top of the wall. On top, he used sheets, tied together, to lower himself down the two-stories. He knew he was very fortunate, because without his friend, he could not possibly have escaped without injury or detection.

Outside the quarantine area, my father suspected police would search for him. He spotted a large, unused water pipe nearby. Crawling into it, he waited, hoping that if police were searching, they would eventually give up.

Leaving the pipe, he began the journey of a few days' walk in the direction of his father's farm. He walked through farms as much as possible, in the hope of not being spotted by authorities.

My father returns to Italy to marry

Sometime after this, my father returned to Italy, perhaps for an arranged marriage. He was certainly in Italy by 1908, when at 26 years old, he married his first wife, Antonietta Di Luzio. Soon after they married, the couple went back to the family in Argentina, where they lived in a house on my grandparents' property outside of Rosario. They grew crops like corn, zucchini and citrus.

Antonietta and my father had three children. The first two were born in Argentina - Isolina in 1910 and Urbano in 1913. Then, sometime between 1913 and 1915, the family returned to Ari in Italy where a second son, Argentino, was born in 1915. I do not know the cause, but it is a great tragedy that the two sons, my half-brothers, died at a young age in Ari in 1915.

Antonietta's ill health

I can only imagine the devastation that the death of two sons had on Antonietta's mental health. She suffered terribly, tormented by memories that could not be relieved by doctors or my father. She deteriorated each passing day until she did not recognise my father. It was very hard for my father and harder for his poor wife.

Towards the end, on the doctor's advice, Antonietta was hospitalised so she could be monitored and supported professionally. She survived in the Teramo asylum only a few months, passing away in May 1925, when she was only 34 years old. She was buried at the Ari cemetery.

It grieves me that the graves of my father, his first wife Antonietta and my mother Assuntina are no longer at the Ari cemetery. Why are they gone? It is a great shame, but that was the way of things. When graves in rural areas were not visited and maintained by family, they were considered 'abandoned' and were removed and reused. Even today, grave plots in Italy are maintained for a certain time and then reused unless a renewal fee is paid.

Sometime before Antonietta passed away, my father went abroad again, chaperoning Antonietta's sister, who was to be married, to North America. He stayed in North America for nearly three years and worked in a coal mine. This is where he contracted the lung disease that would eventually rob us of our father.

For safety reasons in communications, mine workers had to attend English language school. Through this school and with help from the Italian Americans he worked with, my father learned to speak English.

Uncle Giuseppe

Uncle Giuseppe was reportedly a famous high jumper, winning the Argentinian championships at one point. Grandfather and father went along to support him at competitions and even at his training. After years of competing, Uncle Giuseppe opened an athletic training centre in Rosario.

I remember my father's stories that Giuseppe was the absolute boss, although he was the youngest son. He kept my father and grandfather busy, giving the young athletes as much training value as possible. My father became a good athlete himself.

This all happened before he returned to Ari, all before I was born.

Two brothers marry two sisters

Uncle Giuseppe travelled from Argentina to Ari, where he married Anna Salvatore in 1921. In October 1925, following the death of his first wife, my father married Anna's sister, Assuntino Salvatore. Assuntino, my mother, was 20 years younger than my father.

The Salvatore family also came from Ari, and they had four girls and one boy. As a young man, their son, my Uncle Corino and his wife, moved to Africa and opened a shoe factory. The factory produced boots for the Italian army. His wife ran a jewellery shop. After many years, they moved back to Ari which is when I met them.

Giuseppe returned to his career in Argentina, leaving his pregnant wife behind, expecting Anna and the baby would join him soon. For family reasons, Anna and their daughter Natuccia never left Ari, and Giuseppe never returned to Italy. He met another woman and every letter I recall the family receiving, was directed to Natuccia, pleading for her to come to Argentina. After Natuccia married, she and her husband, as well as my Aunt Anna, did immigrate to Argentina. Natuccia finally met her father.

My mother Assuntino Salvatore

My mother was popular in the local village and surrounding area as a high-class seamstress. She sewed for men, women, and children. Her specialty was formal occasion clothes like wedding dresses. I remember her affectionately, watching her spread out material to cut and sew and create high standard clothing. She did not enjoy working on the farm, but her seamstress work was phenomenal and added to our small family income. My parents had two sons, my brother Antonio, born in June 1926, and me, born the following year in June 1927.

My father worked the land in Ari, for possibly five years. Then he went back to Argentina to prepare for us to move there. I was three and Antonio four, when he went away. For two years, my father worked and prepared for us to go to Argentina.

During this time, my mother became very sick, suffering from a stomach problem that could not be diagnosed or cured. A doctor visited her regularly, but she slowly got worse. These were difficult and scary times with my mother so sick and my father away. We survived through the great generosity of Aunt Anna, the local priest, and our neighbours. This is the way the Italian people were, living and working in such unity and care for each other.

With my mother's ill health, my father's plans changed, and he returned to Italy for a final time. Six months later, in March 1933, Antonio and I faced the devastating loss of our beloved mother. She died in our home. My poor father had lost his second wife, again taken from him in tragic circumstances.

My father desperately wanted to settle in Argentina to be reunited with his family. Some months after my mother's funeral, he made plans for us to leave Italy. Fate intervened again. When the travel date drew near, passage to Argentina became more difficult. Argentina, like the rest of the world, was experiencing the Great Depression with its rising unemployment. The Argentinian Government introduced new laws restricting migration. To immigrate, my father would need a labour contract and proof of savings. Then in his 50's, he did not have a contract.

It is interesting how these moments change one's destiny. If we had made that final trip to Argentina, I probably would have stayed there and avoided the devastation of World War II; but at the price of not immigrating to Australia. So it was that my father and Antonio and I, took over my grandparents' lands around Ari and the two houses.

My stepmother, Camilla Assunta Ricci (Assunta)

Not long after my mother died, my father was being treated for his lung condition at nearby Guardiagrele hospital. Here he met Assunta Ricci, the hospital matron, and a war widow. Assunta's husband, Costantino Tinari, fought in World War I, and a firearm wound, which would not heal, eventually killed him. Birth records show that Assunta and Costantino had a daughter Nicoletta, who died at just two months old, in 1920.

As a younger woman, Assunta greatly desired to be a doctor. She completed superior school, but her family was too poor to send her to university for the five-year medical degree. She was very intelligent and could have achieved so much more if there were better academic opportunities for poor, rural people in those days.

Unable to study to be a doctor, Assunta became a hospital nurse and later matron at Guardiagrele hospital. She worked there for many years, before she left to relocate to Ari to be with my father. I was six and Antonio seven, when she came to live with us. My father and Assunta did not marry, I think because the war widow's pension would be lost, but I remember her with great fondness, and she created a family with the four of us.

Assunta was a tremendous help in our community. People came to her with their medical issues. She assisted local midwives when women gave birth. About 13 years after I left Italy, she died from complications with diabetes. Until she lost her eyesight, she wrote beautiful letters to me, almost weekly, in Australia. She died sometime around 1965.

My brother Giovanni Antonio Costantini

Antonio and I were bought closer together by the terrible loss of our mother. Antonio was strong, and one of the most hard-working people I've ever known. He was kind and protective. We did all the things young rural peasant boys did - explore, race, climb trees, and make slingshots (a stick with a fork, with a rubber strap attached to shoot pebbles). As young children, we worked on the farm and as we got older, our workloads increased. Antonio was a great brother; without him, my life would be hugely different and less fulfilled. Many of the stories I describe in this book, we experienced together.

I immigrated to Australia in 1952, and Antonio followed in 1956, arriving on a ship called the 'Sydney'. His wife Giuseppina and their two young boys, my nephews Giustino and Lucio, immigrated a little later, on a ship called the 'Roma'.

They made their home in Sydney, with Antonio working in the Acme bed factory as an assistant spray painter and factory hand. After some time, he moved to the Postmaster General's Department and worked as a cleaning supervisor at Redfern Post Office for over two decades. On weekends he was in high demand for gardening and handyman work because everyone knew he was such a hard worker.

I dearly miss my brother, who passed away in 2018, and my sister-in-law, Giuseppina, who passed away a few years earlier. Their sons Giustino and Lucio are both retired after successful careers and live in Sydney with their families.

My sister Isolina

My half-sister Isolina was the only surviving child of my father's first marriage. Isolina was 17 when I was born, and my memories of her are as a kind woman. She married Luigi and lived on his family farm in Vacri, a neighbouring town to Ari. Isolina and Luigi had three children. My niece, Eufemia, stayed in Italy. She and her husband Mario had two daughters. These are my remaining, dearly loved, Italian family.

Isolina's eldest daughter, my niece, Rosalinda, immigrated to Australia in 1963 when she was in her late teens. She lived with us for two years before marrying Pasquale and moving to Brisbane. With immeasurable sadness, Rosalinda passed away in Brisbane in 2020, survived by her husband and their three children.

Isolina's son, my nephew Rocco, lives in Philadelphia, USA, with his wife Anna and their son and daughter. Rocco lived in Australia for some time as a young man, including in the 1970's in Brisbane with his sister Rosalinda. We saw each other often and became very close. We remain so to this day, talking often on the phone.

My cousins

I have already mentioned cousin Natuccia. She was like a sister to Antonio and me. She married Franco and they lived in Roccamontepiano, a lovely neighbouring township not far from Ari. Natuccia and Franco immigrated to Argentina in 1953, where Franco practised his craft as a skilled carpenter. He was still doing carpentry jobs in his early 90's. Sadly, Natuccia passed away in 2018.

Another cousin, Elodia and her husband Santino (nicknamed Rubano), also immigrated to Australia from Chieti. Rubano left Italy in 1955, and Elodia came with their son and daughter two years later. In the early years of my life in Narangba, when Rubano and Elodia were in Brisbane, we were very close and saw each other often. Whenever Betty and I had to go to Brisbane, Rubano and Elodia would host and accommodate us with warm generosity. They also enjoyed visiting us on the farm. Sadly, Rubano passed away in 1995.

MY EARLY DAYS

From the time of my birth in 1927, to the time of writing my story in 2021, I am grateful to have fulfilled so many goals. My life has been a journey that in many ways symbolises humanity's capacity to overcome and succeed. Through my book, I hope to encourage others to also have hope and to believe that they can also overcome and succeed. From my early life, I have always tried to open my heart and think about humanity. Perhaps because, even as an infant, I had challenges to overcome.

Unfortunately for my brother and me, my mother was unable to breastfeed successfully. Like now and long before baby formula was invented, doctors impressed on women the importance of breastfeeding. They encouraged the use of wetnurses rather than using animals' milk.

When Antonio was born, my mother was unable to find a wetnurse and so he was nurtured on love and donkey's milk. I was luckier when I was born because a local village woman gave birth around the same time and had milk to spare. 10 months after my birth, my mother's sister gave birth to my cousin, Natuccia and from then I was nourished alongside

Natuccia. I tell this story by way of explaining the strong bond I had with my 'second sister', Natuccia and my 'second mother', Anna.

My grandfather's houses in Ari

My grandfather's two houses in Ari were close together. Like most village homes, there were two to three stories, not much space, and built to provide what was needed for survival. We lived upstairs. Downstairs we stored food for ourselves and our animals. In the warmer, sunny weather, fruit and vegetables were spread out in canisters and stored on the rooftops.

There were no fences around our property. Boundaries were divided with fruit and nut trees. We had chestnuts, figs, almonds, olives, cherries and apricots. The trees were pruned to grow properly, animals ate the leaves, and wood was used for cooking and heating. We never wasted anything.

Each of my children have visited Ari and seen the house I grew up in. In 2019, our home was bought by a family from Rome and is used now as a holiday home. The second house in which my cousin Natuccia grew up, was the original family home and much older. It has been abandoned for decades and was a ruin when I visited Italy in 1988.

Our houses were very close to the home of our close cousins, Nicolo and Natalina (children of one of my mother's other sisters). We grew up together, roaming throughout the village and the fruit trees, playing games. My best memories were climbing trees and playing in the snow. Old houses and barns were great for playing hide and seek. I liked a game we called bones or knuckles, known as jacks, here in Australia. We played by throwing up stones and catching them on the back of our hands, starting with one stone and increasing the number until one was dropped. The player who caught the most stones on the back of their hand won.

Early learning

As a child, I was inquisitive and inclined to study. At the Ari elementary (primary) school for five years, we learnt basics of reading, writing, arithmetic and Italian heritage, also essential skills for rural children like simple agriculture and digging water wells. Ari's school had one teacher who taught twenty-five of us of all ages and levels.

School hours of 9am to 3pm were designed to fit into rural life. In summer, these hours left time for morning and afternoon farm work, playtime and study. Daylight went from around 5.30am to 8.30pm. In winter, the sun rose around 7.30am and set around 5pm, so we completed school during daylight hours.

I greatly desired to continue studying, but it was not possible, due to work required on the farms and my father being unwell. Added to that, there was no high school in Ari and further study would have meant relocating to Chieti during the school week.

We could not afford the cost of me relocating to Chieti, or the time away from work. There was another problem which made it impossible for me to attend high-school or university in Rome. Italy was a very religious country and the law required that students have two parents, married to each other. This I did not have. If I had been able to continue studying, who knows what different journey I may have had!

For many my age, we went from finishing elementary school, to working on family farms. While our career opportunities were limited, our lives had many positives. A great value of being in a small village and sharing community life was everyone had a sense of extended family.

On Sundays, most people went to church, and the Priest was like one of the family. He was the first to assess if anyone was missing or needed help. Before every service, he would ask if there were any needs and always made sure people received help when they needed. This Priest's care for others is a lasting inspiration for my life and attitude.

Farming in Ari – memories before and after the war

Most village locals worked the land, producing what was needed for survival. We helped each other and nothing was wasted. When one family had a big load of work, such as threshing corn, others came to help. If one family did not own a donkey, another family lent theirs. Produce was exchanged and people helped the sick and those unable to work.

If someone in the village was good at something, they shared their skills with those who needed it. My father was very good at massage and many people came to him for massages. It was a barter economy, and the community lived and survived together, by staying united and sharing with one another.

Animals were essential to daily life on the farms. We had two cows to work the land and for milking. I remember climbing up on steps to put the cart on the cattle. They wore a yoke on top and harness underneath with ropes to turn them left or right. Young cows were trained alongside older ones so by the time they took the yoke, they were good, steady workers. They ploughed and carried food we grew, like corn and potatoes. We stored manure behind the stables to put back on the farm as fertiliser.

We used a donkey constantly, transporting machinery, supplies and crops in and out of fields. Heavy machinery was hardly ever available and not useful in many cases, as the land was hilly.

In rotation, from the markets, we bought three bulls per year, of different ages, fattened them up, then sold them for meat.

Chickens were kept for eggs and eaten when they were too old to lay. Rabbits were bred, eaten and sold. They lived under the trough for the cows and ran around with the animals.

We had six big, excellent milking sheep and made a tremendous amount of cheese (pecorino) and ricotta from them. The wool, mainly white, was used to make socks and clothes. We had a few breeding sows, and these could have 9 or 10 piglets at a time.

If people owned male animals to breed with, like bulls, rams or boars, they registered them, so that all the community, including the vets, knew where they came from. This way, the quality of stock was maintained.

To breed pigs, we took our breeding sows to the people who were registered, left the animals there and picked them up later. If our animals had male babies, we didn't keep them for breeding. They were butchered for porchetta (roasted whole suckling pig).

The day before 'festa' (party) days, the local butcher killed the pigs and prepared them for cooking. We had a large, wood-fired oven built from bricks underneath the steps in our house. The oven would fit two pigs that we could see cooking. We sold the roasted pork at the feste to earn money.

It was at our local feste that my love for music was born, and to this day I am still singing the Italian folk songs that were part of my youth.

Fruit trees, grapevines and crops were part of our farm life. I already mentioned my father making cane baskets and canisters. All of us helped, first by collecting the best green cane from a patch of cane that we grew for this purpose. Our little patch was tightly packed, reaching up to 3m tall. We could tell by feeling it when the cane was ready to cut, to make stakes for climbing beans and tomatoes, and to make canisters.

Cane canisters were used for many purposes. Apples were stored in them on roof tops in fine weather and fruit was dried in them in our oven. Dried fruits and meat kept us nourished through winter.

Of course, it would not have been an Italian rural farm without grapes, for eating and making wine. Behind our house we grew special eating varieties of grapes that were covered in fruit in summer. We all loved eating these table grapes, making sure we left enough to be dried for winter.

Our patch of wine grapes was larger. We harvested ripe grapes by hand, loading them into big baskets hanging each side of the donkey, maybe 50kg each basket. The grapes were tipped into a special bag then tied up and hoisted by a rope above a large, wooden trough. Antonio and I had great fun, hanging on to two steel pipes installed above the trough, jumping up and down crushing the grapes. The juice was collected in the trough and piped into vats for fermenting and starting the wine-making process.

Leftover grape skins ('mosto') were compressed by a machine then boiled in copper cauldrons to make spirit. The chemist sold us flavours to add to the spirits, making 'grappa'. I was never a big fan of grappa, but many in the village loved it. Whatever was left over from the grappa-making process was mixed into the fertilizer pile outside the stables and put back onto the farm.

We also made vino cotto (cooked wine), which I enjoyed far more than grappa. We boiled the juice until about one-third of the volume had evaporated, then placed the concentrated juice into fermentation barrels. Sometimes we added vino cotto to white wine to make a sweeter drink.

We all drank wine every day. Children drank wine weak in alcohol content, usually made from white grapes. Adults drank stronger wine which we also used as antiseptic for wounds and as medicine. For sore throats, we heated the strong wine and drank it before bedtime, tying a sock filled with warm ashes around our necks.

We had no heating, so coals from the fire were put in a steel plate, with ashes on top. This went inside a box and was covered, then put on our beds to warm them. Before going to bed, the plates were put on the floor which warmed the room. If it was snowing outside, this helped to keep our rooms warm.

My life as a young boy was busy with manual work on the farms. To ignore the work of growing food and tending animals was not an option, as that would mean a loss of the necessities of life. In it all, we always made time for family and community life.

Feste (parties)

It was not a wealthy life for small farmers like us. We didn't have many things that societies today take for granted. But what we had was powerful community spirit and we gathered to celebrate as often as we could. When there were so few options for entertainment, the village people created their own.

After the working week finished, usually Saturday or Sunday night, family and friends united in a pre-arranged household. Musicians played the traditional music and people danced and everyone loved to sing along. Instruments included the piano accordion, guitar, mandolin and violin.

Before playing, musicians nominated 'directors' to start the dancing and make sure everyone got up to dance when the music started. We danced waltzes, the tango and other lively dances. It wasn't possible for anyone to be left out. I greatly valued these times as they involved all members of the community, making us all feel equal. To this day, I have a deep respect for the organisational skills of those directors who made sure everyone got involved.

I have very fond memories of my brother Antonio at the dances. He absolutely loved to dance. Even after working all day, he danced late into the evening. He could have just a couple of hours' sleep and be back at work early the next day.

The dances were also a way for young adults to socialise while being chaperoned. Many rural farmers met their husband or wife at the feste. This happened for Antonio, who, after the war, spent many hours with his future wife, Giuseppina, on the dance floor.

Life was changing in Italy

In school, we were taught that Mussolini was a good leader who created the Italian Fascist party and who, in 1922, successfully opposed a weak national government in Rome to become Prime Minister. World War I had weakened the Italian economy, and we learned that Mussolini would help us. I know now this was propaganda the government wanted us to believe, because while Mussolini did some good, he was a brutal dictator.

Before the war, the government under Mussolini put money into road, medical, cultural and agricultural projects to increase Italy's prosperity. However, his dream of creating an Italian empire led to international clashes. These included his fateful military involvement in Ethiopia; and worst of all, his siding with Germany's Hitler leading Italy into the devastation of World War II. The vast majority of Italians, including my father, had hopes that Mussolini would resist an alliance with Germany, but he sided with Hitler against the will of most of the Italian people.

In his early days as Prime Minister, Mussolini's agricultural projects did improve our lives. He gave farmers access to farming equipment so they could enlarge their crops. For some farmers, this meant they could grow grapes on a large scale. They were given new posts and trellises to grow grapes on. A family friend in nearby Bucchianico, established a large enough area of grapes to pioneer large scale production of wine in this region. Many other farmers did as well, and to this day, growing wine grapes and producing wine is one of the region's most important industries.

Changes were not limited to farming. Mussolini continued earlier governments' work in controlling malaria, improving sanitation, and creating new industries. For rural people, this meant new, non-farm jobs were created, and there was a growing sense of pride in the Italian economy that was so badly damaged by World War I.

However, this brief time of positivity did not last, with Nazis in the north and war on the horizon.

World War II and The End Of Life As We Knew It

Italians and our country suffered badly during World War I, even though Italy was on the winning side. Because of this, when World War II started in 1939, most Italians wanted Italy to stay neutral. Nobody wanted the country to suffer as it had in World War I.

The situation for Germany was very different to that of Italy in the lead up to 1939. After World War I, Germany was very poor due to the costs of the war and the penalties that followed. The people lived in misery, the economy was weak, and their currency worth almost nothing. In this setting, Hitler rose to power by capturing the hearts of the German people with a promise of something better. Of course, there were also many Germans that did not support Hitler, but many did, in the hope for a better life.

This was not the case for Italy, a victor in World War I, fighting with the Allies. Italy had not suffered the poverty that Germany had. Mussolini did not therefore have the same power over the people when it came to capturing hearts, minds, and support for the war, as Hitler had amongst the Germans.

Perhaps this was one of the reasons why Italy was slow to enter the war, finally giving in to German pressure in June 1940, after France surrendered. By September 1940, Italy had declared war on Germany's enemies.

Although supporting Hitler in France, Mussolini also had his eye on expanding Italy's territories in Africa. He had already occupied Ethiopia in 1936. This occupation started an internal Ethiopian resistance against the Italian forces, which festered for many years. Mussolini tried to strengthen his control of occupied Africa, and Greece was seen as a key to gaining safe passage for Italian forces.

Italian forces attacked Greece in October 1940 after already occupying neighbouring Albania. Whatever Mussolini's reasons for invading Greece, it was a disaster. The Greeks fought hard to defend their homeland, pushing Italian forces back into Albania. Greece was only eventually conquered when Germany came to Italy's help in December 1940.

Despite the setbacks in Greece, Italy continued its attacks into occupied Africa, with the occupation itself opposed by the Allies. The Allies defeated Italy in Ethiopia in 1941, marking the beginning of the end for Mussolini. The dictator's support amongst the Italian people died out until, in 1943, the King of Italy dismissed him and placed him in exile in the Gran Sasso Mountains in Abruzzo, not far from where we lived. Shortly after, Italy surrendered to the Allies, joining them in their war against Germany.

But the problem for Italy was that, by this time, the Germans already occupied Italy, welcomed in by Mussolini when he was the dictator. The Nazis gave Italian soldiers a choice to keep fighting with the Germans or become prisoners of war. While some did continue to fight with Germany, most chose not to, and thousands of Italian soldiers were disarmed and either sent to German prison camps or forced into labour camps to help the German war effort.

The Allies, along with Italian soldiers not captured by the Nazis, now fought against the Germans in Italy. It was only then, when the Italian army finally sided with the Allies, that many Italians felt we finally got on the right side in terms of the war effort. As civilians, we were living in a Nazi occupied nation. This is why I have always talked about not being 'liberated' until all German occupying forces left Italy.

My uncles in the war

During the period of the Italian invasion of Greece, two of my uncles, Ettore and Nicolo Costantini, fought in the Italian forces and were on a transport ship to Greece when their ship was attacked. An explosion on the ship shot a splinter into Uncle Nicolo's eye causing permanent blindness in that eye. Both uncles escaped and it was a Greek family who helped Nicolo to find medical assistance. Discharged from the military, Nicolo returned to his family land in Ari.

Uncle Ettore escaped with no serious injuries and continued to fight in Greece, then Africa. When the war ended, he too returned to Ari. My uncles' house was close to ours and after the war, we spoke often about their experiences.

Conflict in Abruzzo forced us from home

Abruzzo was one of the centres of military action because the Germans had key forces located in the region. My native village of Ari was part of the frontline and fighting continued around us for almost 18 months.

Bombs and fighting ravaged our village and region. The area was bombarded by Allied planes and battleships in the Adriatic Sea. Some bombs exploded before hitting the ground and shrapnel burst out in all directions. The Allies also had ground troops that fought the Germans throughout the region.

While the Germans only had a few planes, they did have strong ground artillery with machine guns, anti-aircraft artillery and tanks to attack Allied airpower. No one was safe. This is why so many from the community had to evacuate to caves to avoid being killed by the bombs. Caves were dug everywhere, and many people lived in them, including us - dark holes without light, water, sanitation, or access to sufficient food.

With such intensive Allied attacks, it was a desperate situation for the Germans as well. They also lacked food and provisions and took whatever they needed from local Italians to survive and continue to fight. During these dark times, we often wondered why the Germans kept fighting. It was only after the war that we believe we found a reason. Hitler was a great speechmaker, and we think he convinced his people that German engineering, including the development of an atomic bomb, would eventually lead to victory.

Fortunately, in the case of the atomic bomb, this was not going to happen. The Allies would not give Germany access to all the materials needed for the bomb and they ended up developing one themselves in America.

A frightening experience

Before we were evacuated from Ari, my family and some of our neighbours had a terrifying experience with a Nazi officer. A small group of German soldiers were staying near our house. They had announced they were neutral and were friendly to us and others in the community. They even visited our house. A young soldier visited one day. As was our custom, a container filled with apples, was stored on the roof of our three-story home. The soldier asked my father if he could have some apples. My father responded that no-one could reach the apples, because other German soldiers had taken the long ladder that we normally used.

Not discouraged, the soldier put a short ladder on top of a wine barrel to climb up and get the apples. My father warned him that the barrel might not hold his weight, but the soldier didn't listen. As he was climbing, the barrel broke and the German fell and injured himself.

My father tried to get help for the man from the other neutral German soldiers. However, more soldiers had arrived the night before, including a senior Nazi officer. It was this officer and his men who came to our home. The Nazi officer didn't understand what had happened to cause the young soldier's injury. He accused my father of having attacked the man. My father spoke no German, and the officer spoke no Italian, so confusion was strong. Nazis were well known to have killed many innocent Italian civilians during the war. Our fear was intense. We were in big trouble.

Shouting at us, the Nazi officer lined up my whole family and our neighbours (about 20 of us) and threatened that we were to be executed. With guns pointed at us, we were ordered to face a wall and to keep our hands in the air. Our hearts pounded in our chests. Frozen with terror, we waited for the shots.

Although we stood there for just seconds, it seemed like hours. Suddenly, the German officer ordered his men to release us. Later we guessed that one of the soldiers, a friend of the wounded man, spoke to the officer and explained what had happened. In the days to come, we would experience more times like this where we believe God saved our lives.

My father helps Allies escape

The atmosphere was intense and volatile in our village. One night around 10pm, there was loud knocking on our door. Three men stood outside - two Australian, one French. They spoke no Italian and had been directed to our door because my father was one of the few locals who spoke some English.

My family prepared food for the starving men while my father tried to understand their story. They were extremely grateful they could communicate, being escaped prisoners of war needing a place to hide. Like us, they were hoping the war would end soon with an armistice.

They stayed with us that night, and my father advised them to hide at Ari cemetery where small mausoleums housed remains of whole families. Leaving their donkey with us, the men hid in the cemetery. I was assigned to take food to them, sharing the little we had.

My father instructed me to be careful to hide what was happening from the Nazis stationed in our village. I tried not to attract attention when I took food to the men at the cemetery. This went on for almost six weeks, and then disappointing news arrived that war would continue. We didn't know when, or if, Europe would be liberated.

After this bad news, the men decided to leave Italy for neutral Switzerland. My father drew a map to the nearby Majella Mountain. From there, he advised they travel north, through the Apennine Mountain range towards Switzerland. It was about 12km to the Majella and another 1,000km or so to Switzerland. My father explained that the route through the mountains was difficult and dangerous, but the mountainous countryside was their best chance to avoid recapture by German troops.

One evening, around 6pm, when firing usually stopped for a while, the escapees left their cemetery hideout to start their journey. We sent them off with sincere wishes they would succeed in their trip and reach Switzerland safely. To this day, I hope they did, but we never saw or heard from them again.

Digging in

A few months before we were forced to evacuate Ari, the Allies began to occupy territory nearby. This gave us hope that we might soon be liberated from the Nazis, but it would be another ten months before Italy would be liberated by Allied forces. While we lived in hope to avoid the worst, we didn't know what would happen to us tomorrow.

We knew the battle would soon be on us and the village would not be safe, so we planned to dig a large cave. The carefully chosen location was on Uncle Nicolo's land in Ari. Villagers worked in shifts, using steel bars and chisels, 24 hours a day, for almost two months. These tools were made by our local blacksmith.

When we finished, the cave entry was around two metres high, then opened inside to a height of six metres. The cavity was six metres long, with two caves going off from the centre. The two offshoots provided privacy if a woman needed to give birth and isolation for the sick. At roughly three metres wide, there was space for people to sleep and not be disturbed if someone needed to walk past to exit the cave. There was room for 50 people and if we could refuge there, we would be close to our homes, ready to move back as soon as the war ended. Our work was all for nothing, as cannons were placed near our homes, directed towards the Adriatic Sea, and Allied bombs increased. We quickly made plans to evacuate Ari.

Evacuating from Ari to Vacri

One evening in 1944, forever etched in my memory, the occupying Nazis wrote a notice in chalk on our wall, in Italian. The same was written on our neighbours' homes. The notice read that we must evacuate our homes before 10am the next morning or we would be sent to a prison camp or killed.

No reason was given and there was no time to ask questions. Perhaps they anticipated Ari would be a centre of the frontline and they wanted our homes to accommodate troops. Whatever the reason, we weren't waiting around to find out.

Isolina, Luigi, and their young son Rocco, lived on Luigi's family farm near Vacri. At the time the notice was written on our wall, Isolina and a distant cousin from Vacri, Nicoletta, were visiting to help us relocate to Vacri with them. It was a big help to us that the escaped prisoners of war had left their donkey with us.

My father, stepmother, and brother loaded one donkey to the brim. We packed sacks to carry on our shoulders, as much as we could bear. My brother, stepmother and I hurriedly left Ari towards Isolina's place at Vacri. It was the depth of winter, snowing and freezing cold.

Another close call for my father

My father, Isolina and Nicoletta stayed behind, loading up the second donkey. They were late leaving because my father's watch was running behind time. Not realising, my father thought there were still some moments to escape. Caught after 10am by a Nazi commander, he and the women were seized and taken to a soldiers' station. They waited all day, terrified of their fate. Around 10pm they were interrogated, "Why didn't you obey the requirement to leave before 10am?"

My father showed his watch to prove it was running late. Checking the watch himself, the commander believed my father's explanation. He ordered them to get out before midnight or to face the consequences.

Our relief was so strong when we saw them coming down the road that morning, and we were so happy to be reunited at Isolina's family's place in Vacri. This is where we stayed together after leaving Ari. To my family and friends who have been there, yes, this is the current farm of my niece and her husband and family. You will know 'la casa vecchia' – the 'old house'.

At that time, we felt safer at the Vacri farm than at Ari. Although only a few kilometres away, the place in Vacri is in a valley, wedged between two hills and enclosed on the west by the Majella Mountain. This gave some protection from bombs, whether cannon artillery or from the air. We thought the main risk would be from Allied ships firing from the Adriatic Sea at German encampments.

A small creek runs through the valley at the foot of the Vacri farm. It would be difficult for troops to travel over the hills from the north or south or to cross the creek with heavy equipment. The only entry for soldiers would be from the road or through farms, from either end of the valley. This gave us a little peace of mind, knowing if we had to get away in a hurry, we had a better chance to escape.

For a short while, it was calm. Even so, we dug another cave to shelter and hide in if the fighting front did sweep through or if we suffered heavy bombardment. By this time in the war, Allies had designed a bomb for warfare in hilly countryside or trenches. The bomb could explode in the air just before impact, meaning gullies and trenches could be penetrated. Being in a cave gave us the best hope if the valley fell under that kind of fire. We also knew that at any time, Nazis might force civilians into labour camps as part of their occupation. It was time to go into hiding.

The cave location was chosen not far from the farm, in an area covered in heavily spiked bushes which would help us remain undetected. Even if soldiers passed nearby, we hoped they wouldn't find the cave.

Tensions increased. By the time the cave was finished, it was too dangerous to stay at the house because of artillery fire. A German troop coming through Vacri told us that if we wanted to survive, we should leave. Signs were being posted around the roads, telling people to go now.

Ever hopeful that the Allies were getting closer to winning, we decided to stay in Vacri and sleep in the cave at nights. We were trying to avoid evacuation to a more distant location, because at least the house and farm were a base in Vacri. We slept in the cave at night and hid there most of the day.

The American pilot

We knew we needed an escape route from the cave and started to build a concealed passage through the thick bushes. Dressed in dark clothes made of strong material to protect us from thorns, we worked in the shadows of night, cutting a line through bushes with secateurs.

One night, Antonio (Nicoletta's brother) and I were working on our escape route, and both suddenly froze when we caught sight of movement. A woman, dressed in military clothing, came out of hiding. She tried to speak to us in English, so we signalled her to follow us back to the cave where my father was.

She was an American reconnaissance pilot photographing German military camps to inform the bombing operations. Her plane was hit by German artillery, she parachuted and landed not far from us. She must not have been on the ground long because she was outside in the freezing cold. Now she was in great fear of capture by German soldiers.

My father asked her about the war, "What was happening?" Her answer shattered our hopes for a quick victory for the Allies. The Germans had strong capability for ongoing bombardments against the Allies and the fighting might continue for some time.

The woman gratefully shared our food and slept in the cave that night. My father knew she was in grave danger and would not fare well if captured. Neither would we if the Germans found us helping her.

A plan quickly came together. The priority was to change her pilot's uniform. Isolina gave her some clothes and Luigi buried the uniform. Not knowing where the Allied encampments were, my father advised her the same as he had the other escaping Allied soldiers. Head north via the mountains, towards Switzerland.

She stayed with us until early the next evening, then left with a map and as much advice and supplies as we could offer her. Her journey to Switzerland would be extremely hard. She would have to walk alone, through the mountains. We hoped she found sympathetic villagers along the way or even better, an Allied encampment, but we have no idea how her journey ended.

Nazis kill our neighbor

Days later, we learnt that Nazi soldiers had discovered a cave just 500 metres away from ours. Even though the cave was empty, they had thrown in a hand grenade to destroy it. We heard the explosion.

They found out which family had dug the cave and went to their house. They demanded the women remain inside and the men go with them. The parents of the household had a newborn baby and asked the commander if the father could remain with his wife and child. The commander refused, and the father was ordered out. He tried to negotiate but was shot by a German soldier, following orders from the officer. The poor man collapsed to the ground, killed in sight of his devastated family.

The man's sons were forced to drag their father's corpse out to the street and a couple of kilometres down the road to a crossroads. Soldiers forced them to dig a hole, then to bury their father with his legs exposed, one leg pointing to Vacri and the other pointing to nearby Semivicoli. No doubt this horror was meant to terrify the local people into complete submission.

The next day, the women of the family were forced to walk past the shallow grave. Then they were taken to the Nazi camp where the women were forced to cook and clean. The boys were forced into labour digging trenches and other work. Eventually, they were released.

The good colonel

We continued to hope the end of the war was near. We stuck together, tried to stay safe and helped people when we could. We were all hungry. A close friend with a new baby did not have enough milk to nourish her child so two of the men left the cave to milk a neighbour's cow. They knew the cow was stabled and fed, so they hoped it would provide milk for the baby. The men set out by the light of a small candle. Two German soldiers noticed the candle flickering in the dark and investigated. Thankfully, they were regular army and friendly, not Nazis. They said their colonel was arriving the next day and he spoke Italian perfectly.

We soon met the new colonel and because he was friendlier to us, we felt safe to go back to the house, which made it easier to get food and supplies. We all stayed on the ground floor, believing we might be safer there if bombs hit the second floor.

It was a small miracle during that infernal time to have this good-natured colonel around. It was bitterly cold and raining and snowing constantly, so leaving the cave was a good outcome for us. When we moved back to the house, we had a regular visitor in the new colonel who did speak Italian perfectly.

Speaking our language was not the only Italian thing this gentleman did excellently. He was in love with good Italian food and wine and for about one month he visited our house every day to be fed! He must have really loved the food, because at one point he declared our house to be under his personal protection. He was in command of about 30 uniformed German soldiers, all armed for war.

Nazis take our cousins
Not long after the horrendous death of our neighbour, the Nazi commander responsible and the group he was with, were moved on from Vacri. Another Nazi encampment was based at nearby Turri, so the Nazis were still around, and they brought us more fear and concern.

My cousin, Natuccia, and a friend, both about 15 years old, left the house to search for food nearby. The girls were apprehended by two Nazi soldiers and taken away. In a panic, Isolina went immediately to inform the colonel, begging for his help. He found the girls and the soldiers and ordered the girls to be released and left alone. What relief when the soldiers obeyed then returned to their camp, about a kilometre away.

That was not the end of it. The Nazis did not like being ordered around. Returning with more men, they opened fire towards our house, the colonel and us.

The colonel warned us urgently, "Stay low on the floor!" He returned fire with a small machine gun. Thankfully his men soon ran to our rescue and opened fire, forcing the attackers to retreat. It was strange and confusing, seeing the Germans fighting against each other.

From the different way we were treated by the Nazis and the regular German army, we learned that not all German soldiers were the same. The Italian speaking colonel and his men occupying Vacri were not the same character as the previous Nazis. They engaged with the citizens in a very different way.

After the Nazis attacked their own army, the colonel explained that the frontline was moving, and a large bombardment of perforating bombs was likely to hit the immediate area. The colonel impressed on all the remaining locals that evacuation was the best option. He told us the caves would not provide any real safety and that Nazis would attack anyone who stayed in the village. He urged us to get out immediately.

Evacuation to Chieti

We knew better than to argue and prepared to move on again, this time to Chieti city. Given the German colonel's warning, Isolina's family came with us. It was no longer safe for anyone to stay in Vacri.

It was early spring and still snowing, so we stayed the first night at a vacant house not far away. The colonel had not lied about the bombardment, and bombs exploded all around that very night. A bomb hit the house we were taking shelter in. It tore through the roof but by some miracle, did not explode. Many bombs didn't detonate on impact, and we were very relieved this was one. Years after the war, we lived with the danger of unexploded bombs and land mines. These were a constant reminder of our ravaged land.

The next morning, the bombs had stopped. All was calm. We started walking again, through Vacri township, past Bucchianico towards Chieti.

Along the way, another man and I had gone searching for edible plants and food. Two German soldiers discovered us and suspected we were spying for Allied soldiers. Gripping my nose hard, one soldier demanded we take them to our group. Hoping with desperation that our family would not be harmed, we led them back. To our great relief, we were able to convince the soldiers that we were an Italian family group looking for refuge. They left us alone.

Moving on, we walked carefully along marked paths to avoid unexploded mines buried in snow. We came to a deep creek, raging powerfully from the recent extensive rain and snow. God bless that person who had previously tied a tightrope to trees from one side to the other. Holding onto this rope for dear life and inching along it was the only way we could get across.

Our predicament was intensified because Isolina's three-year old son, Rocco, was with her, and she was more than 8 months' pregnant with Rosalinda. My father carried Rocco across on his shoulders while others helped Isolina. Working together, we finally all stood safely on the other side.

Staying in Chieti

By the time we arrived in Chieti, the German forces had declared it 'Citta Aperta' - an 'open city'. This meant the German's made known they would abandon their defensive efforts in the hope that the city might avoid destruction. We hoped that being an open city, Chieti was less likely to be bombed and we would have a better chance to survive.

I believe the Germans declared three cities in Italy to be open cities during the war: Rome and Florence, hoping to preserve the amazing history of those cities, and Chieti. One can only hope that the intent of kind officers, like the colonel we befriended, did this so rural Italians had a safe haven in a long, bloody war zone.

Being declared an open city did not mean Chieti was liberated. It only meant Germans would not use it as a defensive base, expecting the Allies wouldn't bomb it. Germans still occupied the city and controlled movement to make sure locals were not cooperating with the Allies. For young, healthy men, there was also the risk they would be caught by Nazis and forced into labour camps. This had happened to my brother-in-law, Luigi. While in Vacri, he was forced to work for the Nazi's when he was captured outside.

Arriving at Chieti outskirts, we found an old, abandoned house. We stayed there for a few weeks, knowing Isolina's time to give birth was close. When the time came, it was too dangerous for Luigi to take his wife to the hospital for fear of being captured and taken to a labour camp. My father, then in his early 60's and less likely to be sent to a labour camp, took his daughter to Chieti hospital. This was another sacrifice he made, helping the group stay alive and together. Even though we were apprehensive for the days ahead, what great relief we felt when the birth went well.

Chieti was heavily occupied by the Germans. Times were desperate and food was scarce. Soon after my father and Isolina came back, we had to move on to find food because our supplies were gone. All the while we never gave up hope that liberation would come soon, and the war would be over.

Famine and survival

Discovering a place to stay wasn't hard because many homes were abandoned. The challenge was finding food and provisions. We travelled along the banks of a small river, choosing an abandoned house on the city outskirts. Surrounding farms would be the best places to scavenge for food. We remained in this place for three months, until World War II in Europe ended.

They were a desperate three months. Constantly famished, we were skin and bones. Isolina diminished daily and with so little to eat, she scarcely produced milk for baby Rosalinda. It was a miracle that the baby survived because many didn't.

We stayed alive on whatever we could get our hands on. Every morsal of food was precious. Liquorice trees grew along the creeks, and with the winter snow almost gone, we dug the roots to eat. Raw olives, forest nuts - anything we could find growing or left behind on farms, prevented us from starving to death. Nothing could be cooked because fires were banned so any potatoes we dug up were eaten raw. Sometimes we found flour in abandoned houses or dried broad beans and figs to take back to our family. These finds were treasures of immense value. We ate anything we could find that would give some nutrition.

Every night the men searched for food, but never found enough. On our expeditions, we risked going where we weren't meant to be, but survival was our priority. So many other civilian Italians shared the same struggle, as people came from all over Abruzzo seeking shelter in the open city.

Friendlier soldiers

Even though Chieti was an open city, living on the rural outskirts put us in danger from occupying Germans, and the frontline was still close. Many times, German soldiers confronted us, "What are you doing breaking the rules by being outside the city limits?" Most times, we couldn't understand each other, so we signalled, pointing to our mouths that we were searching for food. I think that being very close to the end of the war, many of these German soldiers themselves were starving and ready to give up.

If not for Hitler's promise to the German army that he was close to developing the atomic bomb to win the war, the German soldiers probably would have gone home long before. By now the Americans and the Allies had more firepower, especially from the air. They had enough planes to cover the air in ongoing formations and the Allied attacks kept coming.

Meanwhile the Germans were running out of means to defend themselves or to mount counterattacks. But the soldiers were forced to stay, right until the end, or they risked retaliation. We knew this because my father offered to help one Italian speaking German officer to escape and stay with us. The poor fellow said he couldn't because Nazis would kill his wife and two children back in Germany if he defected. This would have been true for all regular German army personnel.

Most occupying soldiers around Chieti were kind to us and not threatening like previous Nazis we had encountered. They knew we needed to be out looking for food, and mostly turned a blind eye at this time in the war.

Saved by Contorino Marruccini

While we were refugees at Chieti, one night we had a wonderful surprise. My Uncle Nicolo and our neighbour from Ari, a young man called Contorino Marruccini, came through the door. We had no idea they too were refugees in Chieti, and we were so happy to see them safe and ok. Early the next morning, we set out for our daily forage. Uncle Nicolo and my brother Antonio went one direction; Contorino and I went another.

Contorino and I walked for hours and arrived at a small hill. Close to the frontline, there was some danger of bombs. Empty houses at the top of the hill were our destination to search for food. During early evening, we knew there would be about 45 minutes ceasefire, when the Allies and Germans would stop hostilities.

In that timeframe, we felt sure we could get in and out of the houses. The first house we entered was almost completely destroyed by bombs, but we found four dried figs. We savoured two each, hoping to keep our strength up after no food all day. Outside, tossed into a blackberry bush, we noticed a bottle with a small amount of wine in it. We shared a little wine each but within minutes, I was dreadfully sick and almost passed out.

Whether the wine or figs were bad, or I was just fatigued from starvation, I don't know. Either way, I was in bad shape, struggling to speak or walk. It would not be long before the artillery started again.

Contorino Marruccini was a hero that day. He dragged me down to the gully away from the higher country which was exposed to artillery fire. I don't know how long he dragged me for, because I was struggling not to pass out.

The old man in the cave

We arrived at a low point in the valley, intending to stay for the night. Contorino found a few potatoes which we ate raw. After I rested a little, some strength returned. The night was closing in when we saw a small light nearby, back towards the frontline. We wondered who could be so bold to light a fire that close to artillery fire.

Whoever it was, they were taking a big risk. The mystery turned out good news for us. Following the light, we discovered an old man living in a cave. He was baking bread, roasting potatoes, and cooking beans over a fire! Perhaps because of his old age, he didn't care what the consequences were and if he was going to live (or die) in a cave, he was at least going to eat well! He was very generous to us and that night we ate better than we had in months.

How wonderful to eat roasted potatoes (cooked – not raw!), fresh baked bread and beans. Given the state I was in, it rejuvenated me to have a real meal. What we would have given to share this feast with our famished loved ones. This kind old man told us we could stay with him, but we had to return to our family. We stayed in the cave with him that night and left the next day.

Back with the family, we discovered that thankfully, Uncle Nicolo and my brother had found a lot more food than us, enough to help us survive a few more days yet.

The drunk Nazi

Although it seemed the Germans in Italy wanted desperately to go home and mostly left us alone, one cruel Nazi found his way to our Chieti refuge. He rode in on a large reddish horse and was followed by German Shepherd dogs, which the German army used during the war.

The Nazi entered the house, declaring this was 'his place'. He carried a large leg of ham and a big bottle of vino cotto – or 'cooked' wine which is fortified, heavy in alcohol content. He had already drunk a fair amount because he was obviously drunk.

He kept drinking, and he and his dogs started eating the ham. There was no offer of food or wine for us. With no choice, we stood where we were told and watched with growling stomachs.

For some reason, the drunken officer stripped down to his underpants. Across his back we saw the scars from shrapnel wounds. Our fear rose because he was very drunk and out of control.

Two of our girls walked inside, and I spoke out, warning them that the Nazi was drunk and told them to leave, not guessing that the Nazi would understand Italian. Immediately he became aggressive towards me and staggered for his pistol. I knew I had to run. Rather than take the internal stairs, I ran to the external stairs leading to the second story and jumped down about three metres.

Unhurt, I bolted towards the creek. My brother and other women from our group were searching the creek bank for food, so I ran in the opposite direction to where I knew they were. The German followed me, yelling in German to the dogs to get after me. They were coming towards me, fast.

Thinking quickly, I decided my best hope was to cross the creek, so I jumped in, not thinking about the depth or the strong current. By some miracle (because I couldn't swim!) I made it to the other side. The Nazi stood on the opposite bank, yelling at the dogs to follow me. When they did not obey, in a fury he fired several shots across the creek at me.

I was terrified and stayed hidden all day. Towards dark, I chose a safer place to cross back over the creek and then carefully crept back to the house where I could hear people talking. Other Nazi soldiers had come, and the drunken officer had left with them. With tremendous relief I reunited with my family.

One might ask why soldiers like this cruel man behaved like they did. The acceptance of militarism in Germany at that time was based on Hitler's propaganda, which was fed to the young people. Germans were led to believe they were a superior race, with the right to enforce that image on the world.

Mussolini tried to do the same thing to Italian youth. By forcing people from a young age to adopt the attitudes they were expected to have as adults, they assumed they could control the way people thought and acted.

A different soldier, a different experience

After the incident with the Nazi, again we saw how different German soldiers behaved. Another German soldier arrived at our shelter on a motorcycle. In a bag he carried medication, pain killers and bandages. He was hurt badly, with shrapnel wounds to his leg, and he was looking for help. Specifically, he was looking for my stepmother, Assunta. How he knew where she was and that she had medical experience, I don't know but it was lucky for him that he found her.

After all the horrors that the Germans brought us, it shows the strength of human nature that my stepmother helped this man survive. Even though we were at war and this soldier was on the opposite side, it was her nature and her profession to help him. The grateful man stayed with us for a few days while he healed, and he left thanking my stepmother over and over for all her help.

My stepmother's medical skills in high demand

Perhaps where this fellow went next was a nearby military hospital, because not long after, another two German soldiers arrived. They spoke a little Italian and wanted Assunta to go with them to tend other wounded soldiers.

My stepmother didn't want to go because my father was sick with the bronchial disease and she would not leave him. The soldiers said my father could go with them so she could look after him, as well as their wounded.

This was arranged and they left with the Germans. We didn't know where they were going, how long they would be gone or even if we would see them again. As it turned out, this was about three weeks before the end of the war.

The end of the war and returning home

I was almost 17 when the war ended in Europe on May 8, 1945. When we heard that the horror of the war was over and that the Allies had defeated the Germans, we were flooded with relief and happiness. We could finally return home to our farms.

We were greatly troubled that my father and stepmother were still away when we left Chieti to walk back to Vacri and Ari. Where were they? Were they still alive? Would we see them again or were we facing rebuilding our lives without them? We left with a mixture of heavy hearts for them and joy to be going home. We made it back to our farms without any problems.

After Germany's surrender to the Allies, my father and stepmother left those Germans to whatever their fate was and returned home, on foot, as fast as they could. To our enormous relief and great happiness, they arrived home two days after we did.

At the military hospital, my stepmother's help to the wounded had been greatly needed, and the Germans treated her and my father well. My father was given food and medicine, so his health improved slightly, but after suffering much stress, hardship, and starvation as a refugee, and with the lung disease, he was not a well man.

The massacre at Filetto

After the war, we reunited with other Italians and learned that many lived through horrors much worse than us. At least for us, none of our close family members were killed in the war. Even though this book is about my life, I share a story now that shows the brutality of war and its effect on innocent people.

The story starts in 1998, long after I immigrated to Australia, when I returned to Ari for the first time since leaving Italy. I met with an old friend, who asked if I could take a gift back to Australia and give it to his friend in Brisbane. When I delivered the gift, the man told the story of how he survived a Nazi massacre in Filetto di Camerda, a province near ours. It was when he was a young man that a group of Italian partisans fought and killed some German soldiers. Retaliating in June 1944, the Nazis executed seventeen civilian men from the town, aged 17 years and over.

From the story this man told me, he escaped being killed by lying amongst the bodies and pretending to be dead. I didn't know anything about this massacre and only heard what happened all those years later.

Years after this horror, while visiting the Vatican, this man saw a Bishop and recognised him as the Nazi commander who gave the orders to execute the villagers: Matthias Defregger. He later became Bishop of Munich. It was only later in 1969, the massacre was investigated and Defregger was forced to resign from the priesthood.

Italian Partisans

As you would no doubt have gathered by now, politics was very complicated in Italy in the first half of the last century! Although Mussolini sided with Hitler, he didn't have the hearts of most of the people. Italy had been aligned with the Allies in World War I, and many Italians had no time or interest in Mussolini's goals to side with Hitler's Nazism and the Germans who were enemies in World War I.

From the beginning of the war, the Italian Partisans were heroes who fought against the Italian Fascists and German Nazis. They sided with the Allies well before Italy surrendered and joined the Allies. We knew that during the war, the Partisans helped many Italians escape the Nazis. They were often based in the mountains that ran through the middle of the country, and it was through these passages that the Partisans helped people escape to Switzerland.

Just knowing that the Partisans were fighting for the people, for us, was a relief. As the war drew on, they grew in strength. They were very involved with the Allies in the liberation of Italy during the last stages of the war.

RE-BUILDING OUR LIVES AFTER THE WAR

It was May and the weather was warming up. This was good for us, because many houses in Ari were ruined, including ours, so it would have been hard to stay warm. Allied bombs had done a lot of damage. Our roof was blown off and all the doors and windows were broken. We all worked together, repairing each other's houses the best we could. This was not easy with building materials and equipment in short supply.

Water was scarce too because the aqueduct that brought fresh water to the village from the mountains had been destroyed. We never knew if occupying Germans lived in our home, but they used our well, and because of that, it was not contaminated like others. We knew in some places, bodies were thrown into the wells. The village now relied on our well for its water supply. To make doubly sure there was no contamination, dozens of people worked very hard, emptying and cleaning the well before it refilled with spring water. At least now, the people could work with a song of liberation in their hearts.

Digging up supplies

Before we evacuated, many of us buried materials and clothes in cases. Now we dug these up and used them for sheets and clothing. We dug up our hidden farming tools, cooking implements, copper utensils and large cauldrons used for cooking and wine making. Ours was all hidden on our property beside a small creek. We even hid our plough. It was there after the war, but we had no cow to pull it. Everything was buried in an area covered by blackberries so thorns would discourage anyone from finding our possessions. We were so happy to find everything where we had hidden it, especially our copper utensils.

Copper was in big demand because the German army used it to make bombs. Everything was scarce after the war, especially copper, and it would have been impossible to replace these supplies. Having our materials made a big difference to getting back to normal life.

Welcome help to rebuild

Before the war, Ari had three small chapels, two churches and a small cathedral near the local baron's palace. Around the town, there was an ancient city wall, wide enough for donkeys to walk along it. Parts of the cathedral, the palace and the wall were all destroyed by mines set by the Germans. They did this to make blockades to stop the vehicles of Allied troops. Between the damage to these buildings and people's houses and properties, there were a lot of repairs to be done.

After the war, the Allies, working with the Italian government, were well organised, bringing tradespeople from the northern regions of Italy to help rebuild the southern and central rural areas. Some of these tradespeople stayed on in the region. It was only with this help, funded by the Allies, that many major repairs to people's homes and to the town, were achieved. We were all so thankful for this help.

Back to work on the land

We were all still malnourished and weak, having lost the flesh off our bones, but there was no time to rest because the land and economy were devastated, and we needed to get back to working our farms.

Food was still scarce, and we had to be as resourceful as we could. We all searched for food, while slowly getting back on top of our farms and producing again. We worked together, unified as a family and community. Our hope for the end of the war had come and now our goal was to get back on our feet and back to normal life as soon as possible.

As mentioned earlier, our land was not all together in one place. We had six patches which all had registered names. Legally, this was for paying the rates, but it also helped us to know where people were working. The blocks were called Terminialti, Rossapinto, Vacri, Levalle, Fangacci and the one near our house was Santissimo. Two of our blocks were back towards Vacri. Thankfully, these blocks were not damaged by the bombs.

Here we had orchards of mature trees including cherry varieties, nuts, figs, blackberries and vineyards. They were pieces of land that were truly remarkable, being so fertile. Many of the products we produced there, we could not grow on our other farms.

In other areas, we grew different crops for ourselves and for sale. We had lupins (a kind of legume), lucerne for animals, grapes for food and wine, apples, figs, tomatoes, and beans. We had a couple of mature 'castagne', or chestnut trees that gave us delicious chestnuts for roasting on the fire. We also bought chestnuts from other locals who had more of these magnificent trees than we did. To this day, I love roasting and eating chestnuts!

After the war, we 'rented' other land to provide additional space for farming. No money exchanged hands, as we had none. Rent was paid by us working the land. This block was of great value to us, as it had plenty of water with a stream nearby. Just over half of what we produced went to us and the rest went to the landowner. If a friend had spare land, we all worked the land and shared the produce.

Slowly, during the time between the war's end and me immigrating, we rebuilt our lives. It wasn't easy. One unusual phenomenon was a plague of big black ants. I don't know how widespread this was, but we had never seen it before. Had something in the bombs attracted the insects to breed there? Doors had to be kept shut to keep insects out of homes and every step outside crushed hundreds of them under foot. It was only after very cold weather that they died off.

Our farms started producing the food we needed once more, and eventually we had enough to eat, and some left over to sell.

In spring and summer, my father worked with us on the farm, as his health was always better in warmer months. During winter, his lung condition worsened and he was forced to rest. After the war, my stepmother's military pension re-started, making it possible for her to buy the medicine my father needed.

Healing our land

The farms closest to Ari received the worst bomb damage. Roots of young grape plants were all destroyed. We had to use rootstock or regrow plants, and in some areas whole new vines replaced the old which set us back four years.

To plant grapes, we dug a trench and prepared lines, removed the soil by hand to a meter deep, then replaced it leaving a cultivated strip for planting. The depth gave rootstock vines more chance of surviving in a drought because they could send roots deeper into the earth. The rows were about 50 metres long.

The rootstock was a type of native Italian grape growing wild in the area. It was planted first and allowed to establish. Better fruiting varieties were then grafted into the rootstock. The rootstock was planted as soon as possible, so they could be grafted and start producing quickly. In the first year you may pick one bunch of grapes from a new vine. In the second year, maybe four to five bunches. By the fourth year, it should be producing well.

There were also some vines not as badly damaged on one piece of land about 3km from home. These vines gave us a good amount of grapes that we ate, sold, or made into wine. In this area we had three rows of vines, all spaced with enough room to plant a row of wheat or maize through the middle.

The wheat was never grown in the same place two years in a row, and planting spaces for wheat, maize or other crops were alternated each year. Wheat was cut by hand, tied in bundles, and piled up until the donkeys or cow and cart would haul them home. One agricultural machine went around the farms and as always, the community worked together. The bundles were put into the top of the big machine for crushing. Straw came out from the back of the machine and wheat from the front, then it went into bags. The bags were taken to a mill to crush into flour for making pastas and spaghetti. The straw was heaped in large piles and used for bedding for animals. We and the animals ate the maize.

Self-sufficient

Practically the only food we bought was sugar or fish from the local fish seller. We ate fish on Fridays, according to our Catholic religion.

Our production of chickens and rabbits was re-established. For a long time, there was no money to buy larger animals like cows, sheep and pigs. Not many large animals were left after the war. Before the war, we had two cows to plough and carry the big two-wheeled trailer. Eventually, we were able to buy one, but when I migrated in 1952, we still didn't have a much needed second ploughing cow.

My brother Antonio marries his sweetheart

Antonio decided to marry at a young age, only one year after the war. It was still a very hard time for our family, and we remained desperately poor. We were not very far along the road to full recovery. However, my brother was full of life and enthusiasm, and wanted to press ahead with his life. In 1946, he married Giuseppina Paciocca, from Vacri. Giuseppina's family wanted her to marry someone else, but Antonio and Giuseppina were deeply in love and, as Antonio would say for the rest of his life, he 'stole her away'.

After they married, Antonio and Giuseppina lived with us in Ari, and here, Giustino and Lucio, their two sons, were born. A few years later, Antonio found a nearby house for his family, only about 100 metres from our house.

The aggressive donkey

The male donkey we purchased to help with ploughing and carting was not castrated and he was as big and strong as a mule. He was also bad tempered. We purchased the donkey from Giuseppina's father, who didn't want to sell it to us because he knew it was a biter. Antonio reassured him that he would keep the desperately needed animal under control. Antonio did and never got bitten. But, unless that donkey worked every day, its bad temper flared, and it tried to bite whoever handled it.

Working the donkey daily was impossible when it rained. After a few days in the stable, it became ferocious and restless, with other things on its mind! Putting its straps on when it was in that mood, was very difficult.

One day I was planning a trip into the forest to get wood for our fire in preparation for winter. It was about 5km each trip, with three trips to be made, 15km in the day. The donkey was needed to carry the wood back to the house and there was no issue with its endurance and strength. It could easily carry up to 130kg in one trip. In a day we would have close to 400kg of timber, which I considered a good day's work. I started off early, ready to get stuck into it and all was going ok, until the donkey heard the call of another donkey.

If the other braying animal was female, my donkey would have mating on its mind. If it was a male, a fight for territory might have been brewing. Either way, the stubborn creature was determined to bolt and went crazy trying to get away to the other bellowing donkey. I tried restraining it with a rope, but with great force it swung back, biting me on my side, near my lower ribs.

Not content with one bite, the beast released its frustration and kept coming after me. I was cornered in amongst a small stand of trees with no visible escape route. Luckily three family friends from a nearby farmhouse, heard mine and the donkey's screams and ran to help.

The property owner was a very large man, nicknamed Ercule (Hercules). He yelled out, telling me not to fear and to encourage me in my predicament. He and his men were able to restrain the animal and they led it to his stables. Ercule's wife and daughter bandaged my wound and took me to the local doctor. The bite was nasty and took a couple of weeks to heal sufficiently for me to return to work.

The second time I got bitten by that donkey was the final straw. I wasn't badly hurt, but it was a repeat story. I was leading the donkey out to collect wood for that winter and again it tried to bolt. Again it bit me. That was it for that donkey and me! Uncle Nicolo and I took the ill-tempered creature to the auctions at Pescara which was quite a distance.

Along the way, we were met by a doctor who owned a small farm. He had no sons and was looking for men to help work on his farm. He offered us a job there and then, which of course we couldn't accept. Such is the hospitality of the Italian people, that this generous man and his wife provided us with accommodation for the night, and we shared an evening meal together.

We got to the auctions at Castello Amare and sold the donkey to Gypsies for a good price. I was very glad to see it go. A couple of months later, we replaced the aggressive male with a calm, female donkey, perfect for what we needed.

What a difference it made to our lives to have a better donkey. For village farmers, a good donkey or mule was indispensable because the terrain can be steep and boggy in the wet. Using our donkey as a pack animal was the only way to transport materials or products. As with all things in village life, if one household had a big job that needed more hands or more beasts, help was always on hand.

On our trip to the auctions, we saw the city of Pescara was almost completely in ruins. Little did I know that what I saw there, in terms of the war impact, would play a role in my life in the days ahead.

Short supplies

It took years after the war to rebuild our rural community, because sourcing supplies was so difficult. The fighting had destroyed buildings, businesses and farms that were the fabric of our rural economy. Before the war, we had stored our own seeds each year for replanting the next. After the war, none of those seed stocks remained. A lack of local supplies meant travelling further away to buy seeds of wheat and corn, or to buy tools or animals. My father focussed on how and where to source the needed supplies.

He had heard about an area within the province, not as severely affected, and reasoned that this place may have what we were searching for. We then travelled (with our new friendly, female donkey) in search of this place to buy seeds and a new cow. We asked directions and advice along the way. One evening we knocked on a farmhouse door and it was opened by a lady who lived with her daughter.

We asked if she knew where we could find accommodation and in the incredible generosity of the Italian people, she invited us to stay at their house that night. In the morning, my father explained our need for supplies and resources to re-establish our farms. As we were having a look around their farm, the lady said that she may be able to help. Everyone had been through so much suffering, she said, and it was up to the community to help one another, when they could.

From this dear lady we were able to buy seed stock for corn and wheat. She also had cows, one of which had a calf. We bought the calf which would eventually be used for ploughing fields and pulling carts on our farms. Our spirits were greatly lifted.

We embarked on the road home and made it to Filetto, just outside Ari, at about 11pm that night. Tired and still a long way from home, we asked for help from people my father knew at Filetto. They were happy for us to stay and eat with them. Our calf stayed in their stable, we stayed the night, then finished our journey home to Ari the next day.

The calf grew to be the cow we would use for ploughing. Such a small thing this might seem perhaps today, when most people, in Australia at least, have more of everything than they need. But in the days following the war, it was a lifeline for us to have a working cow once again on our farm.

Near to us was a cheese and ricotta maker who lent us money to buy a milking cow. The cow gave us milk and cheese for ourselves, and we sold excess milk, with only 100 metres distance to transport the milk to a new milk factory. As we sold the milk, we paid the man back.

We were also loaned money to plant tobacco crops. These plants had large leaves, used for making cigars. Again we paid off the loan by selling the crops.

This is how, after the war, families supported each other, and we overcame, and we survived.

Accident with a chipping hoe

A setback to working on the farm happened when I was digging furrows for planting, and accidentally punctured my right leg with a chipping hoe. The local doctor put a plaster on my leg, but after a few weeks, the pain was so excruciating that my stepmother cut the plaster off. An infection had been growing under the cast.

A good friend of my father, with horse and sulky, transported my stepmother and me to a private clinic at Guardiagrele hospital. The clinic was run by a renowned local doctor, Don Palmerino Liberatoscioli. Doctor Liberatoscioli was very unhappy that my leg had been plastered and said the plaster had caused the infection. The best course of treatment, he said, would be Streptomycin, a recently invented antibiotic. The only problem was that the hospital did not have the newly developed antibiotic.

My father contacted his sister-in-law from his first marriage, who lived in North America, hoping she may be able to send the medication to us from there. I never knew how she managed this so quickly, but the drugs arrived soon after by what must have been airmail.

I will never forget those needles in my backside every four hours! Thankfully my stepmother could administer these at home.

My brother Antonio the worker

After the accident I could not work for some time. That's when I realised that our family's survival was in no small part due to my brother Antonio. He was invaluable, working non-stop, with incredible energy, sleeping little, always ready to get up and go in the morning. He worked on our farms, in a local food shop and at the local olive oil factory. He was a force of nature, physically.

One 'quintale' (100kg weight) is, in our region, a standard by which dry goods are bagged, sold, and transported, such as olives, corn, beans and wheat. Actually, it's measured at 101kg, to allow for the bag's weight. Antonio would lift and carry the 100kg bags of products on his shoulders, unloading them off a truck and carrying them into the shop where he worked. Once, when I tried lifting one of those bags, his boss told me not to bother as I would hurt myself! That's what most people used a trolley for.

Antonio wasn't paid in cash for this work, but he brought home bread, pasta, fish, salami and other goods from the shop for our family. Not many men could do what Antonio did. He remains the hardest working man I have ever met in my life.

Growing olives

A book about my life in Italy would not be complete without mention of growing olives and how important olive oil was in our lives. Like all local farmers, we grew olives for oil and for use in cooking.

We crushed our olives at a local olive press in Ari. To crush olives, two large wheels rolled across a big, circular, cement dish. A blindfolded horse, tied to a pole, pulled the crush around in circles, driving the mechanism. This process crushed the olives beautifully, breaking them in preparation to be pressed. After being crushed, a large wooden press was used to extract the oil. This was hard work and a long process. The same approach is used to make olive oil today, except with the latest modern equipment and technology. Our region remains a major source of olive oil that is sold worldwide.

Gypsies

In the warmer months, Gypsies often came through rural Italian villages. Small groups travelled through our village and were allowed to stay for a week, according to local council law. If there were no problems and the community was happy having them there, they could stay longer before having to move on. The length of their stay was up to the local council who could move them on after a week.

In Ari, Gypsy groups camped at local parks, erecting tents or staying in caravans pulled by animals. They sold or traded goods and animals, and played music that villagers enjoyed. They never really worked or took local jobs, because it was not part of their culture to settle too long in one place. They told people's fortunes in exchange for money or goods. Generally, they were honest, and it was not an issue to have them around.

However, some in the community were always wary of Gypsies and with good reason, as some Gypsies did steal things. If a particular group was caught out doing something wrong, they would be pushed out of town and not welcomed back.

I liked having the good-natured Gypsies around. It was something new happening in town and they brought news from other areas. We were always on guard though, and I did have my own encounter with some dishonest Gypsies.

One of our blocks of land had a combination of mature grapes, corn and wheat. It was the grapes these Gypsies were after, and I caught them trying to steal an amount of about 14-15 cases worth. It was a Sunday morning, when most people were at church, and the Gypsies knew that was the best time to get up to mischief.

Our family was aware of these tricks, and when the Gypsies were in town, Antonio and I had a system of checking our land on Sunday mornings. We alternated taking turns going to church and checking the farms. One week I checked the farms and Antonio went to church, and vice versa the next week. On this occasion, our surveillance caught a group of Gypsies stealing our grapes. I yelled at them to stop, but they took no notice of me.

These Gypsies had no idea we Italians had a few tricks up our own sleeves to protect our farms. Local boys, such as me, Antonio, and our close friend from school Nicolo, had an alarm system. We would communicate with each other using a series of loud whistles in different sequences that had different meanings.

When the Gypsies ignored me, I let off the three-whistle signal, as loud as I could, that indicated 'come please - I need help'. Luckily, Nicolo, who lived close to that block of land, was in ear-shot. He got there very quickly, along with his father, his mother, and their dog. The dog, trained for this very thing, was commanded to chase the Gypsies. It went into a ferocious mood and succeeded in doing just that.

We ran those Gypsies off our family's land and saved the grapes from being stolen and eaten or sold by the Gypsies. They took off with their horses and trailers and we never saw those particular Gypsies again. After working all year to produce a crop, there was no way we could allow Gypsies to steal the produce we needed for ourselves, or to sell to survive.

Neighbors hit the jackpot

For a couple of young men, our close neighbours, there was great personal prosperity after the war. It also came at a very high price.

During the war, the families of these boys, like many others, were taking refuge from the Germans and the Allied bombs, in a cave in the hills. This cave was between Ari and Orsogna. One moonlit evening, the boys' mothers noticed activity in a nearby, lower lying area. Off in the distance, they watched two people rolling and carrying a large bottle, seemingly very heavy, given the way it was being carried. The bottle was buried.

The women suspected something valuable had been buried and with their curiosity growing, they went to investigate. Unknown to them was that German soldiers were not far from that area. In the growing dark, the soldiers opened fire. One of the women was killed immediately. The other was also shot but not badly wounded. Staying low, she managed to escape and made it back to the cave.

Like everyone else, these families were soon evacuated by the Germans. After the war, the two young men, most likely directed by the surviving mother, dug up the bottle with its mysterious contents. We would never know exactly what happened next. What we do know is that both men suddenly became extremely rich.

One man opened a new corn and wheat crushing mill and enlarged an existing food shop, already owned by their family. The other bought a small fleet of trucks for carting and tipping gravel used for roadworks. The new businesses were welcome by everyone as they brought jobs and money to the town. This included for my brother Antonio, who worked at the food shop and helped to build a large house for one of the men.

One of the young men married my cousin. He bought a prestige vehicle for transporting diplomats to meetings from Chieti and nearby Pescara to Rome. I worked for him, washing his cars, and he taught me how to drive. There were only four cars in our village at the time.

It might forever be a mystery exactly how these fellows became so wealthy overnight. But everyone in the village suspected it had something to do with what was secretly buried that night to be hidden from the Nazis. Whatever it was, that sudden, mysterious wealth for these families was great news for the people of Ari.

Becoming a Man

As I left my teenage years behind and became a young man, my mind was on what I would do in the future. Working on our land was an option, but I was also interested in a different career.

Italy had a financial police corps called Il Corpo di Finanziere. This was a well-respected public official role. I was aiming for this, largely because of the devastation of the war and because my father had such poor health. Having a professional job would offer more money for my family and help me achieve more of what I wanted out of life.

To qualify to study for this job, I needed a school certificate. Sadly, all our records and documentation were destroyed in the war, including my elementary school certificate, so I had to redo the examinations. I sat the exams with school children at the Ari public school, when I was around 23 years old. After passing the exams, I had what I needed for my future plans.

An obstacle overcome

My goal of entering the training was blocked however, because every young Italian male was required to do two years military service. Because of this, my brother Antonio had gone to the military department in Chieti. After a few weeks, perhaps because of a health issue or because he was married, he was sent home again, so he did not serve in the military. I had no love for the idea of going into military service, or the idea of delaying my plans for two years. I wanted to head straight into study for the public service role.

Fortunately, my father, who was well respected in Ari, knew a retired Italian general who fought with Italian forces in the Italian invasion of Africa. General Don Perino di Felice was a distinguished older gentleman and was considered a respected dignitary of great status in our small village.

This retired general used his influence to help me avoid having to do military service. Therefore, with high hopes and ambitions, I went to the provincial office to make the application for the police corps.

Fate intervenes

However, fate intervened in my plans. A family friend who was the mayor of the local Ari council, visited our farm one afternoon, and asked me if I wanted to go to Australia as a migrant. He told me that if I did, I would have to make an application right away. He said that even if I didn't meet the requirements, I might be able to go to Naples and at least see that great city, as that is where they would make final assessments as to who could go.

I knew a little of this mysterious place called Australia, as I had met Australian soldiers during the war and had learnt a little about Australia at school. I decided to apply, at least to see what happened. With Italy so impoverished, I thought I could go to Australia for a few years, make some money and come back home to help my family. I spoke to my father and my family. My father was not happy and did not want me to go, but my mind was made up to apply.

My father only let me make the application on the basis that if I was accepted, he would borrow money to buy a comprehensive insurance package for me. The insurance money would be deposited by bank transfer into an Australian bank account before I arrived in Australia. With this insurance, he explained, I would be secure knowing that if I got sick or injured in Australia, I would be looked after and would be able to return home. It was only after agreeing on this arrangement that my father let me go to make the immigration application.

The rush to apply

I had one day to organise my application. The same afternoon our friend the mayor visited, he arranged a lift for me to and from Orsogna, where I could have a photo taken for the application. I returned to Ari, completed the application, then had to walk to Chieti, as no vehicle was available. I walked 20km during the night, so I would be there when the immigration office opened in the morning.

I arrived half an hour before the office opened and bought coffee and biscuits while I waited. When the office opened, I submitted my application. A man accepted my application and told me to go home, go back to work, and wait. He explained that only 10 men would be accepted to immigrate to Australia from the 70-odd towns within the province at the time of that round of applications. With that news, I set out for the long walk home.

Seven days passed when I received a telegram - I had passed preliminary assessments and was now able to go to Naples by train for more assessments. In Naples, we applicants were assessed many times by both Australians and Italians. This was a long process and included medicals, x-rays, and a psychological assessment.

I was asked, 'Why do you want to go to Australia?' I explained that our land was decimated during the war, and while we were rebuilding slowly, life was very difficult for my family. I wanted to go to Australia for a few years, work hard to send money home and eventually bring money back, when I returned. I was also asked if I'd had any involvement with the Mafia. You weren't going anywhere if you said anything about a Mafia connection.

After the assessments, I was told, "Go back to your family and job and don't elevate your hopes". My answers must have been what they wanted to hear, because within seven days of returning home, notification arrived by telegram that I had been selected to go to Australia. It took only 21 days from start to finish, for me to learn that I had won the lottery to be one of a few chosen to immigrate to Australia. What a gift. A whole new and unknowable pathway lay ahead. I was terrified and excited at the same time.

All of a sudden, my future looked different to anything I ever dreamed of. My family never dreamed of it either. They were shocked that with only 10 selected from the entire province, I was chosen. My father and I talked a lot and eventually he accepted me leaving when I told him my plan to come back after two or three years.

Another obstacle overcome

The next step was to get a travel passport. The trouble was that the government wouldn't give me one because I was enrolled to be assessed to join the financial police corps.

Once more, the retired general helped me. He came with me to the public service office to explain that my plans had changed. With the general's influence, the department was convinced of the genuine progression of events and my application to the public service was withdrawn. With this obstacle overcome, my application for a passport was accepted.

I will never forget the help of this wonderful man, our friend the general. With no further obstacles, my future pathway of travelling to Australia was set.

Never look back

Did my father have a premonition? With my brother Antonio married with a family, still in Ari working on our farm, did he think that one of us at least would always be there? Maybe as a former immigrant himself, he knew how easy it would be to put down roots in a foreign land, as his own father had done in Argentina. I will never know. When it came time for me to leave, he told me, "Never look back". It never crossed my mind that when we hugged and said goodbye, it would be the last time I saw him.

When I left, the house was filled with family and friends. I was overwhelmed with offers of help and gifts of money that people could hardly spare, to send me off. One gift was a beautiful, expensive watch. Saying goodbye was an extremely emotional time. I adored my family and that alone was so difficult. But I was also saying goodbye to friends who had formed such an important part of my life. We were bonded together before, during and after our time as refugees.

Overcome with feelings of sadness and loss, but also anticipation for the future, I boarded the bus from Ari to Chieti. From Chieti I caught a train to the port city of Bari. It was on 17th February 1952, when I was 24 years old, that I left Bari on a ship called 'San Giorgio' to head to Australia. It took 44 days from Bari in Italy to Melbourne, Victoria, and I arrived on the 1st of April 1952. The 'San Giorgio' sailed through the Suez Canal, and into Aden, Port Said, then on to

Fremantle (Western Australia), before docking in Melbourne, Victoria.

Life onboard

The trip from Italy to Australia was challenging. Leaving Bari that night, the wind howled, and the boat was under great pressure from large waves. I got to sleep but awoke feeling very seasick. With the boat tossing up and down, I was violently sick. It was frightening for a farm boy who was accustomed to quiet village life on solid ground in Ari!

This was the only time I was sick during the 44-day journey, but my stomach always felt on edge which made it impossible to enjoy eating. I lost my appetite and with it, any idea that I might endure such a horrid experience, ever again. I lost 6kg during the trip and the ship's doctor's assurance that putting my feet on the ground again was all that was needed to cure me of seasickness, was little comfort. He was right though. Whenever I got off the ship at various ports, I felt much better! Whatever my future held in store, being a sailor was not one of the options! My father had crossed the Atlantic 10 times in his life, however that was not for me!

Despite my constant state of queasiness, life on the ship was an adventure. Onboard were migrants from all over Europe and many were separated from their families. The majority were refugees, leaving home nations and the economic depression of post-war Europe, towards a better hope. Without exception, every passenger was there with a determination to make a better life than the one they left behind.

Passengers befriended and supported each other onboard, despite the cultural differences. Like me, many thought they would only be in Australia for a short time. I wonder how many stayed forever, like I did.

On the ship I met Giuseppe (Joe) Infante, from Bucchianico, located not far from Ari. Joe was one of the 10 accepted to immigrate. He had a strong determination to work hard in the new land. Joe became my close friend in Australia, and we worked together for many years. Through him, I met our family friends, his nephews, Gino and Camillo De Ritis and their families, also from Bucchianico.

Joe went on to become an electrician in Australia but tragically he was killed when he was working high above the ground on a power pole.

Cutting hair onboard the ship

Not far from our house in Ari, was a local barber shop. Our barber was a close friend who showed me his trade, right from when I was a boy. Because of this, I had learnt how to cut hair and I had my own hair-cutting tools onboard.

Now, onboard the ship was an official barber who charged a fee for his cuts. Not many on board had the money, so there was a need of someone who could provide a free service. I was happy to help people. Haircuts kept living spaces clean because short hair meant less chance of lice or other problems.

Cutting hair was also a way for me to meet people on the ship. I was eager to learn of other people and places, and to hear of their dreams for a better life and a better world for humanity. One group of young Sicilian women only came up from below deck once a day, to eat. They always kept their faces covered and didn't speak to anyone. I wondered if they were under the control of the Mafia.

Our bunks were situated down a steep ladder, beneath the sea-line. It was down below that I would give haircuts, out of sight from activity above deck. After about three days of hair cutting, two of the ship's crew came to pay me a visit.

Unhappy with me giving away free haircuts, they confiscated my equipment. Perhaps they were friends with the ship's official barber. Whatever their reason, they were very rude and told me I would get my gear back when we disembarked.

I set out to see if I could get my equipment back and to keep offering haircuts. I also wanted my razor back because I was used to shaving every day! My solution was to find an officer to see what could be done. This search led me to the second-in-command. What a wonderful find this gentleman was! It turned out he was very interested to meet and talk to me, because he was originally from Pescara, also in the Abruzzo region.

He asked if I had been to Pescara, explaining he had not seen his hometown since before the war because he was always at sea. He was desperate for news and asked what I knew of the scars left on his beloved city because of the war. "Is the bridge across the Pescara River still there? My parent's house is nearby."

I told him that I had indeed passed through Pescara after the war, as this was near where the animal markets were. I explained that the bridge had been destroyed by bombs, as was most of the city. When I travelled through Pescara, the river was only passable by a temporary, one lane bridge. This news greatly distressed him.

Unlike nearby Chieti, Pescara was heavily targeted with bombing raids by the Allies because it was a port city used by the Germans. I believe that about three quarters of Pescara's buildings were destroyed or damaged with up to 6,000 civilian casualties.

After our chat about Pescara, the second-in-command was on my side. He returned my barber tools and told me to continue my work. He advised me to clean up after giving a haircut and to keep everything clean and tidy. I went on as he instructed, but a couple of days later, I had another visit from the same men who confiscated my equipment before.

Again, they took my equipment and this time they threatened to confine me. After further discussion together, they said, "This is a warning, but there will not be another one." Off I went again to talk to the same officer as before. He spoke to the men and my tools were returned. I had no more problem from these men for the rest of the voyage.

Now I was free to cut hair, giving up to 10 a day for men, women and children. It helped pass the time during the 44 days at sea and provided a great opportunity to meet new people.

My new officer friend was always happy to see me and to stop for a chat. One day, he asked if I had ever played 'ping-pong'. I hadn't of course. "Do you want to learn?"

A ping-pong table had been set up for crew and passengers. The officer taught me how to play and over the course of the voyage, we played many times. My game never was as good as his, and he always won. I didn't mind as I was so grateful for our acquaintance.

Trouble before Fremantle

Around 10am one morning, when we were about 20km from the port of Fremantle in Western Australia, we sailed into troubled waters, and something went wrong with our ship. The seas in this area under the surface are known to be very rough.

The captain gave orders to prepare lifeboats and for passengers to be ready to disembark. No-one knew what was wrong and we were all alarmed. Before too long, two steamboats arrived. We thought they would help us into Fremantle, but they brought engineering crew, who came onboard and fixed whatever the problem was. No-one needed to disembark, and we continued to Fremantle where we walked on land for the first time in over a month.

We had a day in Fremantle while the ship was given mechanical attention in preparation for the final stage of the journey, being four days to Melbourne. Some of our money, held by the ship officials, was returned to us for the day in Fremantle. For me, this was 10 Australian pounds, a lot of money in 1952. We were given strict instructions not to spend it all.

It was a magnificent day in the beautiful port of Fremantle. Our small group included an Italian fellow who spoke English, which was a terrific help. We ate fresh fruit and relished the taste of watermelon in Australia for the first time. Without the boat rocking my stomach around, I enjoyed a beer at a hotel, where we also had lunch. We explored the town before returning to the ship that night. Back on board, we left Fremantle, and four days later arrived in Melbourne, where my new life in Australia was about to begin.

Bonegilla Migrant Camp

After disembarking, we were put into groups and my group was taken to Melbourne train station and transported to Bonegilla Migrant Camp. This was the same day we arrived in Melbourne, so I didn't see any of Melbourne city.

Bonegilla Migrant camp was set up by the Australian Government to receive and train migrants and refugees when they entered the country. I believe it was originally built as a World War II army base. The reason we were sent to the camp is because they helped immigrants to find work. The camp was large and there were refugees from all over Europe, now including our group of about 20 Italian migrants. Our new home was in the basic cabins at the camp.

It was a tremendous help to have an interpreter who spoke multiple languages. Questions could be asked and information about Australia was provided. Our interpreter wanted us to immerse ourselves in an English language school that was offered within the camp. I attended the school when I wasn't busy cutting hair (still for free). I was so keen to learn English, knowing it would be essential to make my way in Australia.

Through the interpreter, I was asked if I would work on the railway line as a fettler. A fettler's job is to lay, maintain and check the safety of railway lines. As a new immigrant keen for any opportunity, I said, "Yes!". So did my friend Joe Infante.

After four weeks at Bonegilla, we were sent to Sydney and enrolled in the railway's three-month traineeship which qualified me as a fettler. It was a paid internship and my first opportunity to start earning money in Australia.

At Sydney, we were housed with hundreds of other migrants of all nationalities, at a migrant camp at St Leonard's. The interpreter from Bonegilla was with us, which was a great benefit. He was a brilliant man and so helpful to many migrants. He used his language skills to interpret and teach English to many nationalities. He even took us to our first music show in Australia, to Sydney's Trocadero. What a great night.

One night, my friend Joe and I went to a club in Sydney town to see a wrestling match. One of the men in the ring was a famous former world boxing champion, Primo Carnera, who had turned his hand to wrestling. Primo Carnera was a mountain of a man from northern Italy. He was often so much bigger than his opponents that his long, strong arms provided a winning advantage. He was famous in Italy and all over the world, so it was a real experience for us to see him win his wrestling match that night in 1952.

Eyes open wide

Living in Sydney, I began to learn about life in Australia – so different from where I came from, in so many ways. Those few months in St Leonard's migrant camp were a revelation for me. There were thousands of people there, of different nationalities and languages. I come from a little agricultural village and Sydney was a big, commercial city.

One Sunday, our interpreter told us there was a large religious festival being held in a park in Sydney. He asked if a group of us wanted to go with him, and I was very keen to accept and learn more of this new world. He explained there would be a representation of the Italian Catholic religion, as well as another 12 or so other religions.

My head spun - 12 other religions? I understood that there were other cultures and religions in the world, but coming from the rural, Italian countryside, I had no knowledge of what such cultures and religions might involve. At home we had Catholics – or Gypsies! To see a representation of 12 other religions, all lined up in large tents, one after another, all with their own religious and cultural displays was confusing but also a whole new experience for me.

More hair cutting

While doing the fettler's course, I returned to the camp at about 4pm and started cutting hair until about 10pm at night. Now I could charge a small amount because many residents were working and earning money. The money I earned cutting hair during evenings and on weekends was almost as much as my earnings during the week with the railway services.

At St Leonard's camp, I shared a room with Joe, who also worked on the railways. I suggested to Joe that because I was busy cutting hair, he could do the cooking for us, and I would pay for the ingredients. Joe thought that was a great idea and the arrangement worked well for the three months we stayed there. Now I had even more time to cut hair, and I started thinking about opening a barber shop in Sydney.

As had happened to me so many times now, there were forces at play that led me in a different direction. It must have been around mid-1952 that Australia experienced an economic recession. Jobs became harder to find and people walked in all directions looking for work.

Many migrants arriving around that time found it very difficult to find work. We even heard rumours of one migrant ship that arrived in Sydney and the migrants were not allowed to disembark. I am not sure if that was true, but there were definitely less jobs for Australians and for new migrants.

Determination to succeed

I knew that because of my father's generosity, I held insurance cover for two years which would help me return home if I couldn't make my way in Australia. But I had strong determination to succeed. I wanted to work hard and get ahead, and I looked out for any opportunities to advance myself.

Manual work on the railways was hard, laying down track and sleepers. I had time to think about what I could do in Australia. Maybe work in commerce, with firms that sold machines, cars or farm equipment. Any idea I had would require me to speak English well, so I continued to learn at every opportunity.

Traineeship ends and meeting Ernesto (Ernie)

After three months' work and training in Sydney, I was assigned to work on the railway line at Parkes, New South Wales. Joe was sent to another area. I stayed for only two weeks then was sent to the remote location of Roto, also in New South Wales, to work on the railway line there.

The railway department owned several houses in Roto, where Australian families lived permanently. Our time at Roto was helped greatly by these families, who were appreciative to have the help of hard working, young migrants. As strangers in a strange land, we asked all sorts of questions, using our limited knowledge of English and with help from our English-Italian dictionary. With no shops in the remote areas, supplies were provided to the gangs by the railway department. The Australian families in Roto helped us greatly with ordering these supplies.

At Roto there was a small barracks where I met another Italian, Ernie Ciaschetti, who became my close and dear friend. We came from towns close together, with Ernie from Villamagna, about 4km from Ari. Ernie was a great cook, which came in handy for making new friends in Australia. While we were working on the railways, Ernie was always the head cook on our crews. We enjoyed so many experiences together as young migrants in this foreign land.

Ernie was like a brother to me. His friendship became especially important to me on the devastating day when I received a telegram from my stepmother to inform me that my father had passed away. In my heart, I always thought I would see him again and I suffered terrible grief and loneliness being across the ocean, so far from my family at this time of loss. How could it be possible that I would never see my father again? As well as Ernie, the Australian families supported me through my terrible loss. For many weeks I wore a black sash in mourning for my father.

Introducing Italian food to the Australians

Australians are well known for enjoying food from all over the world. But that fondness was not always the case! Ernie and I helped introduce Italian food to a few Australians when working on the railways in central New South Wales.

Our job was to lay railway track, about an hour out from Condobolin. Our maintenance crew was six men - us two Italians and four Australians.

All the food and produce came from Condobolin, and Ernie, being a great cook, knew where to get the tasty and nutritious food we liked to eat. One day, at the camp site, Ernie was making spaghetti with delicious sauce. It smelt so good, and we were all hungry. We asked the Australians if they wanted to join us for spaghetti. But they all said, "NO WAY! We don't eat that foreign food!".

Not long after, two of the Australians went back to Condobolin, just missing out on a severe storm which damaged the line back to Condobolin. Four of us were stuck out on that campsite. Until the line was repaired, no-one could get to town to buy food supplies.

Thanks to Ernie having stocked up, we had supplies, including more spaghetti! The Australians were running out of food. Again Ernie asked, "Would you like to join us?" Their empty stomachs convinced them, and they reluctantly said, "Ok, we will try some".

Well, that first mouthful was all it took to convert them to the joy of Italian food! They cleaned their plates and from then on Ernie was their best mate. The men shared our dwindling supplies.

Stuck in the bush, with few supplies left, we began to worry. That is until a young woman from a nearby sheep station rode into our camp on horseback, stopped and asked, "Do you need help?". She knew the line was damaged because a gang was working nearby, and she suspected other workers on the line might need help. The supplies she returned with carried us through until the line re-opened. Settlers like her, living in these remote areas, helped each other survive. Wherever I've been, I've seen people's kindness shine through in helping others like this.

From that first plate of spaghetti until the end of that job, those Australian fellows became great mates and stuck close to us – especially when Ernie was cooking! They wanted to know how to make, not just eat, Italian food.

When we had time off, we had a few drinks at the Condobolin pub. Those fellows were great fun and told everyone at the pub they had to try this great Italian invention – spaghetti! They even wanted Ernie and I to start a cafe!

Roto

Roto was an important base for maintaining the railway line because it was used to cart ores in and out of the mines at Broken Hill, about 400km west. From Roto, the ores travelled another 800km to the port at Newcastle.

During our three months at Roto, Ernie and I travelled wherever was needed between Roto and Broken Hill. That's when we learned how harsh the Australian environment can be. Sandstorms swirled and raged through the area, leaving large sandhills behind. When the winds ripped through, the animals and livestock scattered across the line and that threatened to derail the trains.

The steam train engines were fitted with a curved, thick metal bar at the front to help repel sand and prevent stray animals from derailing the train. If there was an obstacle due to sand, the trains slowed down to move through carefully, then sped up again as they passed through.

Sandstorms were a constant problem, so a maintenance crew from the mine regularly cleaned most of the sand off the tracks, using special equipment. Our job as fettlers was to place timber sleepers under the lines and make sure any breakages and faults were found and fixed. It was tough work and tough conditions, but we worked hard and were well thought of as a result.

As we were working on the railway line to service the mining industry at Broken Hill, we naturally started to learn more about the mining. We saw it was a huge and important operation, mining many minerals including silver, lead, zinc and even gold. We talked about going to Broken Hill to work but were told that to work there, we needed a very high level of English, which we didn't have. We stayed working with the railway.

Broken bridge on the way to Broken Hill

I have no idea how many years Broken Hill was in severe drought before we got there, but the situation at the time was desperate. One day though, the skies opened, and a storm came through with a great volume and force of water. The rain brought flash flooding that damaged an important rail bridge.

Our six-man crew was the only crew available to repair the bridge quickly. We worked non-stop for two weeks to repair the bridge and the tracks across the bridge. Even though we finished that job, there must have been problems with the line in other places. It was another three weeks after we fixed the bridge before the trains started running again.

Trouble with my eyes

Towards the end of the bridge repair job, my eyes became red and swollen with infection from fly bites. I needed medical attention.

The problem was, the nearest doctor was around 100km cross-country to the south at a place called Hillston, or 400km by rail to the east to Parkes. The train was not due to be operating for another 10 days, so I tried to keep working. My eyes got worse and aggravated me immensely. After six days of my suffering, our Australian gang leader and his wife took pity on me and decided to get involved.

As the train was still not functioning, the only choice was to get to Hillston. This was only achievable with the help of these kind people who drove me cross-country in their T-Model Ford. They were taking a real risk as the flood waters were still high and we had numerous, risky creek crossings along the way. We left at about 3pm one afternoon and arrived at about 9am the next morning.

At Hillston medical centre, a doctor looked at my eyes and gave me medicine that reduced the pain and inflammation. He remained concerned however and told me that I should see an eye specialist in Orange. The next day, we returned to the railway camp base.

Living in a remote area, the only people that can help you are the ones near you. I considered myself very lucky for the help of these people, who happened to have a car, which was quite rare in those days. Without them, I would have been in very difficult circumstances for sure.

Getting back to camp, I could not work due to the need to care for my eyes. I was annoyed at not being able to contribute to the work of the gang.

Within a few days, the train recommenced operations and I made the journey of around 500km to Orange. I arrived at night, coming at the time a large football game was on. Because of this, there were many visitors from out of town and all the hotels were full. I asked around if anyone knew of accommodation that might be available for the night.

Eventually, I met a helpful Polish immigrant at a hotel, who said he had a room in a house in town. He said he would be happy to help me out with a place to stay, given the circumstances and the issue with my eyes. He was a great guy and strongly believed that 'we immigrants need to stick together and help each other when needed'. That suited me, and we went to his house where I looked forward to sleeping after my long journey.

After a few hours of sleep, I was woken by noises in the house. One of my host's Polish 'friends' had turned up very drunk, and had started a fight with him, there obviously having been some issue between them. It was a hell of a fight and I did not get involved. They yelled at each other in Polish, of which I understood not one word. I began to realise that outback towns could be wild places.

My Polish host prevailed, sending the aggressive drunk man away. Then he was very apologetic to me. I managed to get some sleep before seeking out the specialist the next day. The doctor examined my eyes and told me to continue with the medication. He gave instructions on how to care for my eyes and mentioned the possibility of lingering damage.

He also advised that the extreme dust and sandstorms around Roto would not be helpful to my recovery and that I should look for other employment if I could find it, rather than continuing where I was with the railway. I returned to Roto with the intention of moving to a more suitable location.

My Aboriginal encounter

While at Hillston, I had my first understanding of the difficult circumstances facing Australian Aboriginal people at the time. As I waited to see the doctor, I was strolling up and down the street to pass the time, and to take my mind off the irritation and worry of my eyes. I was approached by an Aboriginal man, who had been working quite hard, chopping wood nearby.

He asked me if I could do him a favour and buy him some beer and wine from the local pub, as he was still busy, he explained, and needed to finish his work. "Yes", I said, happy to help him. He gave me money and off I went to the pub to buy him wine and beer.

Well, how naive I was! When I got back to where the man was waiting for his beer and wine, I also encountered the local police sergeant, who was in a very bad mood. He asked me why I was buying alcohol for a black man and told me in no uncertain terms, that it was against the law for a black to buy alcohol, or have it bought for him! He confiscated the alcohol and warned that if it happened again, I would be charged!

I explained as best as I could in broken English, that I was just in town waiting for a medical appointment and was doing the man a favour while I waited. I told him that, as a new immigrant, I had no understanding of that law and certainly would not make the same mistake again!

For a young European, this was a very strange circumstance and a real shock to be caught in the middle of this situation. I had never encountered the idea that one man may walk into a pub and buy a drink, and yet another may not, based on ethnicity; but such was life in outback Australia in the 1950's.

Heading to Condobolin – NSW

After another couple of months at Roto, Ernie and I found work on a 14,000 hectare sheep farm near Condobolin, which produced wool, meat, and grain. This was one of the biggest farms in the region, always with plenty to do. The grain was ready for harvest, and workers were needed.

One job we had was stitching up sacks of grain that had been harvested and bagged by a machine. We loaded the bags onto trucks for transport back to storage sheds. Then we travelled with the bags to a local distribution centre and unloaded them, ready for sale.

When it was time for the sheep sales, we helped muster sheep on this and other properties. We loaded shorn wool onto trucks for transport and cleaned the shearing sheds after shearers finished their work. Much of our work involved clearing land by pushing and burning stumps. Ernie was also the cook for the shearers. We worked six days a week, doing whatever was needed.

One of the amazing things about the grain sheds was the snakes that were welcome to live there. Farmers bought large carpet snakes, which we quickly learned were harmless, to live in the shed to control the mice which chewed holes in the bags to eat the grain. I am certain these snakes were well fed and did a great job as there was not much mice damage. There were also five dogs whose job it was to control the rabbits.

In Ari, we worked land that was so fertile that a few hectares provided food for many. Living and working on this huge station was a great new learning experience.

The Englishman

Ernest Malcolm was an English migrant who lived and worked on the station as second in charge. Most Saturdays he drove a small truck into Condobolin, with Ernie and I on board, going to buy provisions for us and the other farm workers. We stayed all day at Condobolin, and Ernie and I often enjoyed a glass of beer, then a movie at the local cinema.

I didn't know it at the time, but I learned later that Australians swore like mad (but not in front of women and children). We didn't take offence when they swore at us because we didn't know they were swearing at us! They would laugh and then we would become friends. In the pubs, we learned that if you didn't want to fight, you went to the lounge room to eat and drink a beer. If you did want to fight, you sat at the bar.

Riding in the truck with Ernest, with plenty of time to chat, we came to understand a little of his past and how he ended up in Australia. He was previously a landowner in England with his wife and a son. At one point, he became seriously ill, and believing he was dying, signed ownership of the farm over to his wife. Ernest recovered, but sadly, his marriage broke down. When this happened, he was left in a predicament, without a farm or a home.

He decided he couldn't stay in England any longer and immigrated to Australia where he found work on this wheat and sheep farm in Condobolin. As an experienced farmer, Ernest could operate all the necessary machinery. He lived in the main farmhouse along with the station manager. Ernest started to drink alcohol heavily, to cope with the circumstances of losing his farm in England.

After the shearing season finished, the workers had a big party to celebrate, then they moved on. The farm manager, Lloyd, was on his way to Sydney by train, to marry his fiancé, so Ernest, Ernie and I were the only ones left on the farm.

In the early hours of the morning after the party, Ernie and I were woken by a scratching at the door of the shed where we slept. We thought it was a cat but when we opened the door, we saw an injured Ernest. He crawled to the door after a tremendous fall from the veranda of the shearing shed. Landing on rocks, he was badly injured with lacerations and broken bones. He had been drinking heavily and we were worried about internal bleeding. We needed to get him to medical attention urgently.

Well, what a predicament! We had to get Ernest to hospital in Condobolin, but no-one was around to help with transport. Fortunately, Lloyd's new car was locked in the garage, as he had gone to Sydney by train. Ernie had some skill in opening locks without a key and managed to get the garage door open. Once inside, we knew where the keys were kept.

Getting Ernest into the car was difficult as he was so badly injured. Ernie eventually pulled him safely into the back seat. Luckily, I had learned to drive in Italy, even though that was on the other side of the road. I didn't have a license, and this was my first time driving in Australia. Ernie stayed with Ernest in the back to help keep him steady.

We drove to Condobolin hospital, where a doctor said Ernest would need to be admitted for several days to recover. After that we should return and pick him up. We explained we had no telephone or way to be contacted because the farm manager was away for an unknown period of time. We returned to the station with the car, and Ernest stayed at the hospital. He was unable to do anything for himself and needed care and attention.

When we got back to the station with Lloyd's car, who should be there, but Lloyd himself! He had forgotten important documents needed for the wedding and had to return to pick them up. He had taken a train to Condobolin and a taxi from the train station back to the farm. He saw me driving his beloved car and became furious, accusing me of stealing it. He was yelling at me, saying he was calling the police to arrest me.

I waited for him to finish until I could explain what happened. I asked, "What would you do? Ernest would die without help." When he knew the story, he calmed down and said he would have done the same, and we became good friends again.

Ernest eventually returned home and after many weeks, recovered enough to start to move around and take care of himself. It took a couple of months for his broken bones to heal. Ernie and I supported him as much as we could, cooking his meals and helping him bathe. After his accident, Ernest gave up drinking. He was very grateful to Ernie and me for helping him and told us we were like his sons.

More farm work

At the end of the shearing season, Ernie and I went to work on another farm, owned by the same family who owned the sheep and wheat station. This farm had large herds of cattle, a large flock of sheep and grew small crops. Here we met an Italian man from Sardinia, Leonardo Murrudo.

The farm was based on rich soil and had a good water supply, being situated on the Lachlan River. The river was full of native fish that were excellent for eating. We stayed in huts along the river.

Together, we worked incredibly hard and the three of us grew an enormous amount of beans, tomatoes, capsicums, potatoes and lettuce. Leonardo arranged with the manager to sell the produce locally in Condobolin and we would be paid when the produce was sold.

This was my first experience of the heartbreak of small crop production. At the time we needed the farm truck to take produce to market, the manager was involved in an accident with the truck, resulting in it being written off. Without transport, we were unable to sell our produce. Our venture failed, we did not get paid, and it was time to find new work.

Ernie and I moved on to another farming opportunity and Leonardo went to Condobolin as he had an idea to start a cafe. This didn't happen, and it wouldn't be long before we saw Leonardo again. Leonardo and I became very close friends and many years later, I named my youngest son after him.

Grape Farmers

With this failed small crop venture behind us, Ernie arranged another opportunity of growing grapes on a property about 30 miles outside of Mildura. He thought this might be a chance for us to get ahead because the owner was looking for men to operate as share farmers. Once again this meant sharing in the profits when produce sold. We boarded a small plane from Parkes to Mildura then went on to meet the property owner to organise starting work. This is when I found out I was not only bad with sea travel, but also with small plane air travel, being sick on the way.

We arrived and met the owner, his wife and family, and it was agreed that Ernie and I would take on management of the vineyard in Mildura. That region is exceptional for growing grapes, and with our farming experience we were confident we could produce a successful crop.

Like so many things in life, you don't know if you will succeed until you give it a go, but grape farming turned out to be another failed venture. This time because, as we found out, our host had mental health problems from his experiences as a soldier in World War II.

When he was ok, he was great, and we had many interesting conversations, including about the war. I remember his views on how stupid Mussolini was for invading Africa. We had no disagreement on that point! But when he was unwell, he could be abusive and violent. This is when I realised that war not only affected victims like we were, but also the victors like this poor returned soldier.

Our host's wife tried very hard to convince us to stay on, but we were not prepared to be abused, so we left after just a couple of months.

Grape champions in Mildura
We found ourselves in Mildura city with the challenge of planning our next move to find work. Our money was very low with not being paid for our last two jobs. Our next grape working adventure in Mildura was much more successful, and

Ernie and I even won a week-long pickers' competition which earned us £30.

On this new farm, we worked for one picking season. Every day, we started picking when we could see the bunches and stopped when we couldn't see the bunches. Between us, we picked 2-300 cases of grapes a day. Ernie was the muscles. He hoisted the cartons onto the tractor which I drove to dunk into a dipping solution. Then the bunches were spread out on large wooden trays before packing for market.

We were a great team and were excited to win the competition from all the pickers in the local area. These competitions were a clever idea of the farm owners because it meant teams worked harder and faster trying to pick more grapes than the other teams.

North Yallourn coal mine

After this work finished, Ernie and I weighed up our options and thought about heading to Tasmania where we heard there was work in mines. Ernie wanted to go to Tasmania, but I wasn't keen to go back up in a plane again!

In the end, we headed to Melbourne and applied for work everywhere we could. Soon, a short-term position came up at a coal mine in North Yallourn, 150km southeast of Melbourne, so off we went.

Ernie and I really enjoyed working in the mine. It was hard work, but a great experience. The wages were good which lifted our spirits, plus it was cash in the hand. Good meals were provided, so we did not have to cook for ourselves. After work, several of the miners got together to play music which we greatly enjoyed.

There was also an English language school where migrants were assisted in improving their English. Ernie and I took full advantage of this opportunity. One of the mine managers was an Italian man who looked after us and taught us many things about the mining industry. I also started to offer free haircuts to other workers which helped build friendships.

Burrinjuck Dam – drilling explosives

After three months at the coal mine, we heard about work offering at Burrinjuck Dam, on the Murrumbidgee River, near Yass in south-western New South Wales. Major works were required to repair and strengthen the dam wall, which was originally built in the 1920's. It was a difficult decision to stay or go as the work was good and our manager wanted us to stay. But the work at Burrinjuck Dam was paying 50% more than the mine because it was considered dangerous work. In the end, we decided we were in Australia to get ahead. In early 1954, we farewelled our friends at North Yallourn to look for work on the Burrinjuck Dam project.

We got to the dam site and went to the office asking for work. It was explained to us that we could both have a job, but at that point in time, there was only a need for drillers. So, we began working as drillers for dynamite and gelignite explosives, used to produce rock base. The rock base was crushed then used to reinforce concrete for the dam walls.

The drilling involved working on ledges on sloping rock walls that we accessed by wearing special belts and being lowered down the cliff face on ropes. We drilled into the rock face ledge and put dynamite charges in place. Once we were on a certain ledge, we firstly drilled, using a variety of drills in stages, to achieve a depth of about 6-8 metres for each hole. With the holes done, we climbed back up the ropes to the top of the ledge to get the charges. Then we did this again, working our way down the rock face to the ledge, so we could put charges in the holes, ready for blasting later.

The area of rock face to be blasted was around 4 metres wide and 8 metres deep and needed up to 20 charges in that section of rock wall. To start, an expert would also be with us on the ledge, supervising the correct placement of the charges in the holes and connection of the fuses.

Eventually, we became experts in explosives, and could manage that task ourselves, getting everything prepared for blasting by placing gelignite into the holes. We connected wires that linked gelignite charges together and then to a single wire connected to the detonator. This line united the detonator with all the charges and that was the last stage of preparation for blasting.

When everything was ready to go, another expert detonated the explosives once the site was cleared. A loud bell sounded before detonation and care taken to make sure everyone was away from the blast site. The bell also notified everyone at the mine to expect a blast so the workers would not be shocked or frightened.

Once blasted, the rock would fall to the bottom of the pit where massive loaders loaded the rubble onto trucks to be taken for processing into cement. Then we began work on the next ledge to be blasted.

We did this work for around 10 months. By then, enough material was sourced for the repair work required on the dam. After the blasting work, we were involved in building the massive frame needed to fix the dam wall in preparation for concrete being poured to shore up the wall. After the wall was repaired, we worked on constructing the concrete safety barriers along the top of the dam wall.

The work at Burrinjuck Dam was good for Ernie and me. We were learning a lot and soon became thought of as capable operators. This is how, after a couple of years working at Burrinjuck Dam, I went from drilling the holes for explosives to being a work crew supervisor.

In our time off while living at Burrinjuck and working on the dam, we Italians would go to the nearest local town, Yass, not far from Canberra. One of my room mates at Burrinjuck, was an Italian named Guillermo, or William, in English. William and I purchased a new car together, a small 1953, two-door

Ford Anglia, which would become a big part of our future experiences. Ernie in the meantime had purchased a motorbike. All three of us would go to Yass to the cinema, dining and listening to live music.

The Burrinjuck dam repair project eventually came to an end and the work teams finished up too. It was time to look for a new opportunity. We had a great party with the whole work crew when we finished and said our goodbyes around May 1955.

Failed timber cutting venture

As our time at Burrinjuck Dam was coming to an end, Ernie and William decided to pursue different opportunities. Ernie wanted to join his brother at the Snowy Mountain Scheme, and William wanted to investigate a timber cutting contract in Queanbeyan, New South Wales, not far from Canberra.

I decided to join William, which meant we had to find our own truck to cart timber to the sawmill. William and I went to Sydney for this reason and verbally agreed with a dealer to buy a 10-tonne truck. After this, we travelled to Queanbeyan to finalise the terms of the timber cutting contract with the sawmill. But when we went back to Sydney to buy and pick up the truck, the dealer had reneged on the agreement. Most likely he got a better offer, and we had no written contract to hold him to our agreement.

After the failure of the timber cutting venture, William and I decided to join Ernie and his brother and find work on the Snowy Mountain Hydro-electric Scheme. We knew that migrants from all over the world worked there, building the infrastructure to redirect water from the Snowy Mountains, using several dams to create hydroelectricity. Water was then supplied to the Murrumbidgee Irrigation Scheme.

As it often has in my life, fate intervened. It turned out our little car was not suitable for the roads in the Snowy Mountains, with their potholes, bogs and large rocks. This concerned us, and our paths changed again as we learned of an opportunity to cut sugarcane in Ingham in North Queensland.

With sorrow, William and I said our farewells to Ernie, the terrific friend who I had shared so many new experiences with. We kept in touch, and afterwards when I visited Sydney, we saw each other. Ernie and his brother became experts in concrete construction and went on to create a successful contracting business and did very well for themselves as new Australians.

Cutting sugarcane in Ingham, Queensland

Before he worked at Burrinjuck, William had already spent a season in Ingham cutting cane. He became a ganger (supervisor) of a cutting team. This was helpful as he already knew the ropes. So it was that I moved to Ingham in late winter 1955 to cut cane.

These days, sugarcane harvesting is all done mechanically. Back then, every stick of cane was cut by hand, using a sharp machete-like cane knife. We cut cane from July to October, working hard because we got paid by the volume of cane that we harvested. We lived in a timber cottage that had tank water for drinking, but no electricity. For cooking and lighting, we used carbide fuel. For washing, we started a diesel pump and used bore water. We only had a short time to cut the cane, between heavy rains, so we worked long hours, which left us with little time to do anything else except cook, clean and sleep.

In those days, the cane fields were burnt before cutting the cane. The fires got rid of snakes and rats and made it easier to cut the cane; but it caused erosion and removed nutrients from the ground.

Our clothes always stunk like smoke and no matter how much we bathed, so did we! The sugarcane smoke left a sticky cane residue that stuck to our clothes and skin. A lot of time was spent washing ourselves and our clothes before the next day's work came around.

Many of the sugarcane farms in North Queensland were owned by Italians, and they still are today. Most were immigrants who started as cane cutters and stayed on to eventually own their own farms. Whether they stayed in the cane industry or not, Italians and other immigrant workers in the 1950's earned reputations as reliable and hard workers.

The hard work, snakes, blisters, and choking smoke that were part of life on the cane farms were not for everyone. One newly arrived Italian man, who I met in Ingham, learned that because of the language barriers he was not wanted at the farm where he thought he would be working.

I invited him to the farm where I was working, thinking he might join our crew. He did but only lasted a few hours. Not being used to physical work, his hands blistered and bled from using the machete. I think his one cane cutting experience was enough to convince him to return to Italy.

In North Queensland around this time, not many young immigrants had a car. The car I owned with William gave us the wonderful freedom to travel around.

One day, William was driving in Ingham when he had a car accident. He was in hospital for a couple of days. The car was badly damaged, and we were told it would need to be sent by train to Townsville for repair because no one in Ingham could fix it.

The cane season was almost over because heavy rain had reduced the quality and price of the cane. Like many other Italian immigrants, I decided to travel to Mount Isa in Western Queensland to work in the mines after the cane season. William wanted to travel south to escape the heat.

We agreed that I would buy out William's share of the car. The problem was that progress in repairing the car was slow, due, we were told, to parts being sourced from England. Because of the delay, I travelled to Mount Isa before the car was repaired.

At this time, volunteers and workers from the Italian Consulate were available to help immigrants. In Townsville, I benefitted greatly from a wonderful Italian lady who worked on my behalf to have the car repaired. After many months, this kind woman notified me that the car was ready to collect. I returned to Townsville as soon as possible to collect the car. To this day, I am not sure if I would ever have seen the car again if not for that wonderful lady.

I still did not have an Australian drivers' license. It was only after working at the mines for a few months, that I obtained my licence to drive legally.

Mount Isa – working in the mines

It was late in 1955 when I travelled to Mount Isa. Because of my training and experience with explosives, I was offered work at the mine. Even though I was experienced, I had to complete three months of paid training and then have my skills tested before I could begin work. Passing the test, I started work as a miner, working deep underground on different jobs.

There were nine men in our team, and we worked together in threes, in 8-hour shifts. The team worked 24 hours a day, with men swapping over when each shift was over. Sometimes I would be driving the train that carried the ore, another day driving a loader to unload trucks, another day drilling and preparing explosives. The jobs were rotated between all the work crews.

The mines at Mount Isa were a huge operation with around 1,000 men. Even in those days, health and safety was a big issue. With so many workers, there was a need to know which section each worker was in underground. All the work sites had large boards which held a card for each worker, with that person's number. Each man had to flip his card to show when he was in a certain area. When he left that area, he flipped his card back again. If you went to the canteen, you flipped your number, indicating you were in the canteen and not underground. When you went back to a certain work section, you flipped your card back again. In this way, if there was a major incident underground, like an explosion or a collapsed shaft, the management knew where people were and could work out who might be trapped or missing.

The mines were huge underground spaces of great height. In each section, large conveyor belts operated 24 hours a day, carrying ore out of the mines. Once extracted, ores were smelted into blocks, ready to be sold in Australia and overseas.

The pay at the mines was based on how much material was extracted. Teams that extracted more ore than others could earn more money. My teams always did very well.

One of the things I still remember, was how bad the food was at the mine canteens. To be fair to cooks, it would have been difficult to provide good meals with no fresh ingredients or fridges. Meat was all preserved, and hardly anything was fresh.

At the time, there was a mine cafe outside the mining areas, but not enough time to reach the cafe when working underground. On days off I was able to visit this cafe. The menu was one meal only – steak and eggs! I thought it was just great, as the food was all fresh.

During my time at Mount Isa, with other Italian workers, I lived in a private house owned by an Italian family. I studied English three nights a week and continued cutting hair in my spare time for extra cash.

Little did I know that a work accident one day, just as I was finishing a shift underground, would change my life at the mines. An Irish fellow asked for help to lift some heavy pipes. While we were carrying them, he was unable to hold his end and dropped the pipes. I broke two fingers and strained some muscles, making it impossible to do my normal mining work.

The management gave me jobs I could manage while my fingers healed. This included painting machinery and fitting air ventilation and underground water pipes.

There was no workers' compensation in those days, and even if there was, I would never have heard of such a thing. If you were lucky, as I was, management would find suitable work while injuries healed, so injured workers could keep earning money.

I really enjoyed the pipe fitting work and the opportunity to learn many useful fitting and turning skills that would serve me well when I returned to farming years later.

Like many migrants, we worked hard to save money. Some we sent back to our families and some we saved for our futures, whether it be in our new country or back in our old countries. For me, it was to be in my new country, Australia.

Meeting my wife Betty

Shortly after I arrived in Australia in 1952, I began corresponding with Assunta, a young Italian girl from my village. We exchanged letters for about four years, and for a young, homesick migrant, I valued this connection to my home.

Time passed and our correspondence became more than just news from home. With blessings from both families, we agreed to marry by proxy. The marriage would take place in Italy, with Assunta there and me in Australia. My brother would stand in my place. A proxy marriage would mean Assunta could migrate to Australia as my wife. I was going to marry a girl I hardly knew.

Leading up to the marriage date, my sister Isolina developed serious health issues. She needed an operation, and her recovery was going to be long. Because of this, the wedding was postponed, and a new date would be set after Isolina recovered. I believe it was destiny that this marriage never went ahead. Assunta's heart was in the old country, and she met a man from there and got married.

For me, in mid-1956, I met a beautiful woman called Betty Putland who would become my wife. Betty grew up on Magnetic Island near Townsville. We met when she was working at a shop in Mount Isa, which was owned by her sister Lorna and brother-in-law George McGregor. I was shopping for supplies when we met, and after that I found many reasons to go shopping!

Near the end of 1956, the summer Olympic Games were being held in Melbourne. Lorna and George planned to go and while they were away, Betty looked after the shop and Lorna and George's three children. Betty was a hard worker and my friend Leonardo and I helped her where we could.

Our relationship deepened and Betty and I married at the Catholic Church in Mount Isa in January 1957. Lorna was matron of honour to Betty and my friend Leonardo stood as my best man. Australia was now my home - our home.

Betty was trained as a midwife, and she has always cared for people. She loves babies and children and many times she helped mothers in our neighbourhood who were in trouble and needed help. As well as bringing up our five children, she stays active with our grandchildren and now the great grandchildren. She is an inspiration - a hard worker and a wonderful woman, wife and mother.

Time to leave Mount Isa

Mount Isa was good to me – I met my wife, and I had a good job. I was happy to stay there and hoped to take an opportunity to buy a house with attached apartments for workers' accommodation. Mount Isa was a boom town and accommodation was in high demand. Despite our jobs and good prospects, we did not have the banking history needed to secure the large loan to buy the properties. After this fell through, Betty and I began thinking about other opportunities.

During my time in Mount Isa, I sponsored my brother, Antonio, to migrate to Australia, with his wife Giuseppina and two young sons to follow as soon as possible. To sponsor meant applying to the Australian Immigration Department and promise security for migrants when they arrived in Australia. By the end of 1956, Antonio had arrived in Sydney and soon found work. It had been more than four years since we were together, and I was so eager for us to be reunited.

In March 1957, we farewelled family and friends in Mount Isa, and were on our way to Sydney. Townsville and Magnetic Island were our first stop.

Before being in Mount Isa, Betty worked as a midwife in Townsville. Her mother, also named Lorna, and two younger brothers, Frank and Rex, still lived in their family home on Magnetic Island. After we were married, Betty was keen to return to her home and introduce her new husband to her family.

Because the Ford Anglia was so unreliable, the first part of our journey from Mount Isa to Townsville was by train, carrying Betty, me, and our car. From Townsville, we caught the ferry to Magnetic Island. Betty always said she grew up on an island paradise and she was right. We used this time with family to relax and made plans to move to Sydney, both to reunite with Antonio and to look for work.

Our journey to Sydney was long and hard because our car was still causing trouble. After a couple of hours driving, it overheated and we stopped for a couple more hours to let it cool down before starting off again. Because of this, it took quite a few days to get to Sydney. We camped near the road along the way, which was a common thing to do back then.

We finally made it to Sydney and stayed in Antonio's small, rented house, right near a railway line. When the trains came past, the whole house shook with the vibrations. This was not a problem during the day, but at night it was impossible to sleep well!

How wonderful it was to have my brother in Australia and to be united with him again. He was working hard as always, five days a week and on the weekends with the goal to bring his family from Italy to join him. I was impressed with how Antonio had settled into life in Sydney. With him being so busy, plus the shock of being in such a large, noisy city, after a few weeks Betty and I decided to return to Queensland.

At that time, Betty's oldest brother John and his wife, also Betty, were living in a rural area on the outskirts of Brisbane called Narangba, on 4 hectares of land. We decided to go there while we planned our next step.

With great sorrow in leaving Antonio, but enthusiasm for leaving that little house by the railway line, we set off for

Narangba. As it turned out, once we got there, we never left, and we are still here after 64 years!

Narangba and the farm

We stayed with John, Betty and their son Billy, in their one-bedroom house, close to the small town of Narangba. Narangba had a train station, primary school, small shop and a few houses. We lived on a dirt track that ran through the native bush. The track connected Narangba to Old Gympie Road, which was at that time the main road from Brisbane to North Queensland.

At the time, John's Betty was pregnant with their daughter, and my Betty was pregnant with our first child. Our bed was a mattress on a door, which we put over the bathtub in the bathroom each night.

After a short time, we bought a one-hectare block of land from John and Betty, a little closer to the town centre. All together, we stayed with them for about three months. We spent our days making a start on our new house on our block, which eventually grew into what the family now calls 'The Farm'.

The first thing to do was build a toilet! We laid a slab of cement then put up three and a half asbestos walls, a door, and an iron roof. A wooden toilet seat sat on top of a pan which needed regular emptying. There was no toilet paper, just square cuts of newspaper threaded onto string and hung up. A bottle of Phenyl was kept handy for disinfecting. After we got the septic, the little outhouse was used as the kids cubby, and for garden storage.

We had no luck to find a builder to build our house. Builders in Brisbane refused to travel all the way out to Narangba. In fact, one man said Narangba was the end of the world and advised us to sell and move closer to town! Today, Brisbane's boundary extends well past Narangba, but back when we settled here, about 20kms of bush and farmland separated the two.

There was no choice but to start building ourselves. We bought basic materials, including cement and bricks, and collected sand and gravel from the roadsides. House construction started. We moved into our house at the stage where we could put roofing iron across the brick walls to give us basic protection when we slept. If it rained, we tried to sleep in the car. Our first child Anthony (Tony) was born while we were still living under the tin shelter.

Two problems we had in the early days were poisonous snakes and hordes of mosquitoes. Later, when we got a cow, we burnt cow manure by the piles, trying to smoke away the pesky, biting insects.

Back to the building, a kind neighbour, Angus McPhail, made and fitted our doors and windows. I would have liked his help with the whole house, but he ran a farm and delivery business with no time to spare. We were very grateful for the help he did give us.

As the family grew, so did our home. When we first finished building, our house was 30 feet square with a kitchen, lounge, fireplace and two bedrooms. Over twenty years, more rooms were added. Our home served us well, but when it came time to retire, we thought about making it more comfortable. This time, a builder did the work. He expanded the living area, added back and front patios, another bathroom, my music room, and a laundry.

While this was going on, Betty and I once more slept a little rough. We moved into a large garage that was used for storage. The garage was a big block building with a lined ceiling. It was designed to be converted into a granny flat and perhaps a home for one of our children. Many years after we used it as a temporary home, our sons, Tony and Len, converted it into two apartments. For now, my daughter Linda and her husband Iain live in one apartment, and farm workers stay in the other one.

Back to 1957 when we first moved to Narangba, John and Betty wanted to return to Townsville after their daughter was born. We bought John and Betty's other three, one-hectare blocks, agreeing on a value of about 600 pounds. We paid using most of our savings and the Ford Anglia, which gave John and Betty transport to Townsville.

Nearly six years after emigrating, I became a landholder in Australia. Even though we had no town water (which came many years later), or electricity (which came two years later), it was our land, and it was our vision to become farmers.

BECOMING NATIONALISED AND BUILDING THE FARM

Like my father had said, there was no looking back. Australia was now my home. When I arrived, government policy was that migrants had to work for three years before they could be nationalised. This policy encouraged people to settle and work in regional places.

With the help of my old supervisor at Mount Isa Mines, I gained the work record documents and applied for citizenship. My application was successful, and I was nationalised in Caboolture, at a ceremony with the Queensland Premier, in December 1958, six and a half years after setting foot in this new country. To become an Australian citizen, I needed to renounce my Italian citizenship and swear my allegiance to the Queen. With the love of my old country in my heart, this was a difficult thing to do, but even so, it was with pride and hopefulness that I took this oath. Today, all my family are Italian citizens, but I am not!

After buying the land, our savings were almost gone. Our challenge now was how to build a working farm with the money we had left.

We depended on rain for our drinking water supply and couldn't catch water in a rainwater tank until the house roof was built and gutters put on. In the meantime, we used roofing iron structures to run rainwater into containers. When the roof was finished, our next challenge was to set up water for farming.

A small dam was on the property when we bought it, but we knew water supply was very important to farming and decided to build a well as soon as possible after the house was built.

John Sackley, the father of our nearest neighbours (Joan and Tom Bergman and their daughter), divined the spot for our well in a tea-tree swamp area with a shallow depth to groundwater. We made the well with a circumference of about one-and-a-half metres and about ten metres deep. The first three metres was soil and under that was seven metres of sandstone.

I placed gelignite into holes that we dug with a shovel, or by chipping into the sandstone with a hammer and chisel. Working with long fuses to give us the ability to stay away at a safe distance, I detonated just enough gelignite to loosen the soil and rock. We excavated with me in the well filling buckets, and Betty hauling the buckets up to empty them. The sides of the well were lined with bricks to keep the hole stable. It took us about one month to reach a depth that provided good water.

After all our labour, the underground water was too salty for our crops, but the hard work wasn't wasted. Now we had water for baths and washing clothes, and years later we used the well water when we got a septic toilet. We still needed reliable water for irrigating crops, so we decided to make the dam bigger and rely on dam water for farming.

After securing a water supply, our next challenge was to prepare the land for farming. The original eucalypt forest had been logged, and the property was covered in stumps and regrowth trees which were too small for building or milling. Around a third of the land was low-lying tea-tree swamp.

Without heavy machinery, I used gelignite again, blowing stumps out of the ground, then winching them into a burn pile. The wonder is in those days, a carton of gelignite could be bought over the counter of the hardware shop in Strathpine. Imagine being able to go to a hardware shop today to buy such powerful explosives! We also could buy poisons over the counter and most of the ones we used, like DDT, have long been banned because of their danger to people's health.

With dam water and the land cleared of stumps, we needed equipment to plough soil and carry produce. We bought a small second-hand, 'International' tractor to prepare our land for crops.

After this purchase, we bought a truck to transport produce. Sadly for us, in this, the lawyer we used to buy the truck, seemed to be working against us. This was the same lawyer we used to buy the farm. Like many people do today, he added a 'n' to our surname on the deeds, spelling it 'Constantini'. To borrow money for the truck, the bank wanted the deeds to prove we owned the land. The bank told us the spelling on the deeds needed correcting. I visited that lawyer many times, but he would not fix the spelling or give the deeds to me.

This was a great concern because we needed to borrow money to buy the truck to get our produce to market. Without the transport, we would surely run out of money. I often wondered if that was the lawyer's thinking – ready to take over our land if we couldn't afford to keep it.

The Italian Consul recommended I use another lawyer to get the deeds and correct the spelling. This was a success and now with the loan approved, we bought a second-hand Dodge International truck. It usually took very strenuous turning with the crank handle to get it going.

Now we had everything we needed to grow our first crop – potatoes. It was a bumper crop! Finally, our farming career was taking off! It was just our bad luck there was a potato glut in the market that year, so no demand. By now, after all the costs of buying land, building the house, and setting up the farm, our money was almost gone.

We ate potatoes for breakfast, lunch, and dinner for months. So did our dog, Lulu, the neighbour's dogs, our chooks, and anyone who we could give potatoes to! After six months, I said I would never eat another potato! Memory is powerful though, and it was only a few short years before this, when the rare potato, found in an abandoned field, was a treasure of great value, in those war days back in the old country.

Determined to make farming a success, we persevered with small crops like pineapples, strawberries, cucumbers, and gherkins. The crops did well, and we made money when the markets were good. In this time, we welcomed our first daughter and second son.

In the early years of establishing the farm, I also worked at the Royal Brisbane Hospital in the laundry services. Even though the staff treated me so well, my stomach could not handle the site of the blood-covered sheets so after six months, I left.

After that, I worked delivering bread for a local bakery in Petrie. The struggle I had here was every customer's name had to be written down by hand. It took me hours longer than what I was being paid for because of the writing. Already working morning to night on the farm, I did not have enough hours available to keep up the delivery job. My decision to leave was final after a dog bit me during a bread run.

With my experience and fettler qualification, I found work with Queensland Railways, building a new railway line between Narangba and Caboolture. This job lasted for two years and through it I met many wonderful people who would be lifelong family friends.

A family reunion

I was not good at writing letters, but I corresponded with Isolina in Italy, as best as I could. Through these letters, I learned that Isolina and Luigi believed that if Rosalinda immigrated to Australia, her life opportunities would be better than if she remained in Italy. So it was decided, and with great pride I sponsored our niece to immigrate. In April 1963, 19-year-old Rosalinda arrived at our farm in Narangba and stayed with us for two years. She was a strong young lady and worked hard on the farm, helping us enormously.

Having Rosalinda stay with us was one of the happiest times of my life. It brought into our home a part of my family from Italy. It reconnected me to my culture and solidified close harmony with my Italian family that is still strong today. Betty loved Rosalinda too. She was like another daughter, part of our family and our hearts from the minute she arrived.

I was re-invigorated making sure Rosalinda unified in her new country, including with the Italian community in Brisbane. We visited friends and family and went to Italian music concerts and movies. Before long, Rosalinda settled into new life in Australia. A volunteer tutor came each Saturday for a while, to tutor Rosalinda in English. She learned quickly because Betty and the children did not speak Italian. Whenever I could, I also joined in the lessons, always being motivated to improve my English.

When Rosalinda arrived, our house was two bedrooms, a small kitchen and a living room. With three young children and Rosalinda, we needed more room, so we enlarged the house adding another bedroom and a covered area outside, with a septic toilet. This replaced our old bush toilet.

When Rosalinda's English improved, Aunt Elodia found a job for her at the Golden Circle Cannery in Northgate, where Elodia worked. She worked there and kept helping us on the farm until she and Pasquale (an Italian migrant from Calabria) married in 1965 and moved to Brisbane. I was so proud to give Rosalinda away on her wedding day.

It is a great comfort to me that I had family, Rosalinda, Pasquale and their three children, living in Brisbane. Our hearts were broken when Rosalinda passed away in 2020.

The tractor accident

One of our neighbours was preparing his paddocks for planting, when he visited me and asked if I would use my tractor to pull a stump for him. He had dug all around it in preparation. I hooked up the stump and as I was pulling, the old International's wheels sunk into wet soil. The front wheels lifted off the ground, and in bare seconds the tractor tipped over backwards, carrying me with it and leaving me no time to react.

Next thing I knew, I was immobilised with my arm pinned between the steering wheel and the ground. The blood circulation was cutting off and I worried that the bog hole I was in, could seep full of water. Lying there trapped, my anxiety was rising when I heard a voice call my name and say, "Michael, don't worry, nothing is going to happen to you. You are protected." The voice washed over me, and the fear of what would happen to me disappeared. Can you imagine! In the middle of this catastrophe, I knew I was going to make it out ok. To this day, I believe this was God's voice and it brought great peace to my heart.

Thankfully, my eldest boy, Tony, was close by with his friend, Bill McPhail. Tony ran for Betty who called an ambulance and

Bill found the town mechanic and asked him to bring a winch. The mechanic winched the tractor up enough for my arm to be freed. My ribs and arm turned black and blue with bruising, and it took one month before I fully recovered, but I knew I had experienced a miraculous escape that day.

There is never a good time to have an accident, but this was especially bad timing because the farm was in full production. Just like in the old country, friends and neighbours gathered around to help. Betty could not drive, but she worked nonstop to manage the farm, and our friends drove the truck to take crops to the cannery and markets.

After I recovered, I went back to work on the railway. Betty kept the farm running during the day. At night we packed our produce, and weekends were busy with farm work. Our eyes were always open for new income opportunities, and one grabbed our attention when we were in conversation with our neighbours, Owen and Evelyn Campbell.

The Campbells had a small crop farm and a small business raising chickens. The chicken business seemed profitable, not so affected by weather, pests, or market prices. We decided to dive in, and our journey of growing chickens started.

Growing chickens

With the farm still producing crops and me working on the railway, we started our new venture on a small scale. To begin with, we farmed laying chickens, but soon we decided broiler farming (meat chickens) promised a better financial outcome.

We were very excited when we purchased our first batch of around 100 chickens. Before the sheds were built, our second bedroom was used as a night shelter for the chickens, (plus our goat Margarita and her twins Romeo and Juliet).

We bought day-old chickens and they came out in boxes on the train. The boxes had holes on either side so chicks could eat food through the holes. The main thing was to get water to them quickly. They stayed in the boxes for four days. Imagine the relief when we expanded into the bush sheds and didn't have to house share with the animals!

Whether in Italy or in Australia, as we all did for each other in those days, neighbours helped again. Coming back from the Kallangur markets one day, I was driving our truck down McPhail Road and saw a man on the roadside. He was trying to remove a stump using a chain and winch. I stopped to say hello and, happy for a break from work, he asked me in for a cup of coffee. Ozzie Palman was a north Italian immigrant, with about 70 acres on McPhail Road, Narangba.

Ozzie wanted to clear the regrowth timber and stumps to plant strawberries and run a milking cow. I told him that my tractor and I were available to help him. Most of the round timber for our chicken sheds came from Ozzie's place and some came from a friend on the railway. We cut and carted logs to the farm and started building our first sheds.

Using rough timber and second-hand materials from a demolition yard, we built bush sheds for our first few years of growing chickens. Often, for up to three nights in a row, I worked until midnight, building by the light of carbine lamps. After three late nights working, the fourth day I'd have an early night to rejuvenate. On the nights I took produce to the Roma Street markets, I left in the truck around 11pm to be there by midnight and out by 1pm. Life was busy and full.

We invented ideas to make the bush sheds work well. We designed a monorail to help us with feeding, and this simple invention saved a lot of back-breaking work. Feed came in one hundredweight (about 50kg) bags. These were heavy to carry, and it was hard to walk between chickens to put out feed. Our monorail was a 1.5m x .75m rectangular metal bin, hung on two rollers that moved along an angle-iron channel. On this monorail, the bin was easily pushed through the sheds. At the highest point, we installed a chute where feed bags were emptied into the monorail bin.

Gravity helped push the bin down through the sheds, following the fall of the land. When the bin was empty at the bottom, it was pushed back to the top. Betty fed the chickens during the day, often keeping her eyes on the children at the same time by letting them ride in the bin. The system worked well. The new sheds we would eventually build had automatic feeding systems which removed the need for manual feeding.

Drinking water for the chickens was pumped from the dam. My pipe fitting work in Mount Isa mines came in handy to build the water reticulation system in the sheds. The job was constant, as any form of animal farming needs care and focus on the health of the animals.

When we started growing meat chickens, they were crossbred between white Leghorn and Australorp. By the time we retired, we were told chickens were a mix of 13 breeds. The old sheds held about 14,000 birds each batch, and it took around 15 weeks for chickens to be fully grown after which they were sent to the abattoirs.

Convinced that meat chicken farming was a better source of income than cropping, we visited the National Australian Bank in Petrie, hoping to gain a loan to expand. Here, I met the bank manager who would become one of the most influential men in our lives. He greeted me with open arms then listened intently to my idea to build bigger chicken sheds on our farm.

When I asked if I could borrow some money for this project, he told me that first I would have to open a bank account. I said that I would, but I only had a few coins with me. He said that would do, and then and there, we opened a National Australian Bank account.

I asked for a loan of £600 to buy a feed tank and building materials. He replied that he didn't think that would be enough and loaned me £1,200 to get the job done properly. With this, and the help of family and friends, we built more bush sheds.

For years, from that moment on, our National Australian Bank Manager was always behind us, backing us when we needed to take another step forward. With his support, I was able to buy equipment, build new sheds, and purchase other properties in Narangba, which we have since sold.

All through my journey I have been helped by people like this gentleman. He trusted me to work hard and stand by my word when it came to paying back the loans. Finding people like this was a great joy to me and I will never forget him or the friends, neighbours and family who helped us on the property. In this way, communities around Australia developed and prospered – same as in the old country.

The chicken industry

Chicken growing was a good industry but had some problems. When we started with Red Comb (a chicken growers' co-op) we still had to buy the chickens privately and then pay for the feed on top. We ran up big feed bills with Red Comb. Red Comb only paid us for the chickens when they were ready for market. Because it took about three months for chickens to mature, cheque payments were scarce for us.

Many times, we were a long way in debt before we got paid. With that pay, we had to cover living expenses and business debts, plus keep enough money for the next batch. We worried in that waiting time between when chickens were old enough for market and when we got our cheque. Food bills became so high that many farmers went bankrupt, but with our other sources of income, we kept going.

Red Comb itself was struggling financially, and one time, they told us they couldn't take our batch. What would we do with 14,000 full grown chickens and no payment coming for them?

We looked frantically for a new market. With great relief we found a Chinese provider and were paid. After that, I joined a new chicken growers' association, set up by many other growers, with the aim to improve security and payment with Red Comb. This association was good representation for growers, and I was involved for years.

Red Comb's financial problems got worse, so we started growing for Ingham's Enterprises who provided a better deal for growers. They supplied the day-old chickens, food, medication, and spray to use in the sheds between batches. This was a great advance which took massive pressure off growers. We provided the sheds and raised the chickens and Ingham's provided everything else we needed, including debeaking chicks before delivering them.

Before we started with Ingham's, we debeaked each chick by hand ourselves. Using a foot pedalled cutter, the tip of the top beak was cut off so birds couldn't peck one another. They pecked other chicks if they were a different colour or if there was any blood showing. In the case of blood, we sprayed the area with a blue solution to stop cannibalism. Debeaking thousands of chicks was a long, slow process.

At one time, a trial injection called 'caponising' was given when chickens were half grown (therefore much harder to catch). A hormone tablet was injected in the head of every chicken, but the hormones made the birds fat and lazy, so we didn't keep going with that.

Before we started with a co-op, private buyers came out to collect the poultry. One small abattoir owner brought his cattle dog to round up the birds. Betty was glad for that cattle dog because it meant she didn't have to help catch and load chickens on the truck. Later, chickens were always picked by men in trucks, always at night when the birds were quieter and less likely to be stressed.

Between batches, the shed floor was covered with clean newspaper, hanging feed bins were replaced, and water troughs prepared. Tony and Linda were excellent helpers with this.

Singing to the chickens

Ingham's created a payment pool out of which growers were paid. In one week, the company would pick up chickens from several farms. The farm who produced the heaviest weight chickens was paid more out of the pool than the other farmers. We topped the pool often and mostly stayed up near the top.

Many growers rang me to ask why we were doing so well, and some accepted our invitation to come and see. I think a few things helped our success. From our experiences in the old sheds, we learned what worked well and what didn't. I also spread more food out for the young chicks than was required, so wherever they wandered, they could eat. One secret I gave to our visitors was I always sang and talked to the chickens. Whenever I did, the chickens came and ate at my feet.

After years of growing chickens well in the old sheds, Ingham's asked us to expand to meet the growing demand. With our bank manager's backing, financing the shed was not a problem. Time was the problem.

Our family was now five children, and with Betty so busy with the children and farm, and me full-time on the railway, we didn't have time to expand, especially if we had to keep feeding by hand. Thankfully, the new shed would be automated and was very advanced for our industry.

In early 1970, we built the first automated shed with local Irish builder Bill McCausland. Bill was another great friend and a true professional, and the shed was built with no complications. It held over 15,000 chickens, more than all the old sheds put together.

From then, chicken food was delivered to large hoppers and distributed mechanically throughout the shed. Water tanks fed the drinking troughs. The chickens still needed attention and care, but the work was far less manual.

The industry was growing quickly, changing from old-shed technology to new and Ingham's wanted us to build a second new shed to replace the old sheds. Most growers wanted the opportunity to expand, and we thought it was an offer not to be missed.

One obstacle was the new shed had to be built in 44 days, to fit Ingham's chicken hatching schedule. The other was that it was 1974, when Australia was experiencing the largest trade union strike in the country's history. Something called OPEC, a group of oil-producing countries, pushed oil prices up very high. Inflation shot up and unions wanted more pay for their workers. Hundreds of thousands of workers went on strike around Australia.

We started building when prices were going berserk and finding workers was next to impossible. I was ready to work with Bill McCausland again, but he had another contract. Bill did what he could to help, including arranging a shipment of timber from Tasmania, for the trusses.

I was in big trouble. If I couldn't get the shed ready in time, I risked losing the contract with Ingham's. That would send us bankrupt, given what we had borrowed and spent in preparation for the shed. I had no option but to leave my job on the railways and work seven days a week to construct the shed, chasing down materials wherever I could get them.

I dug the holes for the foundations by hand and hoisted each truss using a tractor and borrowed winch, then set the trusses in concrete. I needed to at least get the brooding area ready to meet Ingham's timeline. The 'brooding' area is a small, heat-controlled section of the shed where day-old chickens go when they arrive. After a few weeks, chickens are large enough to be let out into the whole shed.

After the trusses were done, a man visited me. Bill Sullivan, with his wife Lyn, recently arrived in Queensland from Sydney, and he was looking for work. I took him on straight away, without a second's hesitation. Bill was a skilled tradesman and he worked hard. Together, we just made the timeframe required to receive the first batch of chickens into the brooding area. These few weeks were very stressful, but in the end, the shed was finished and everything worked out, with great thanks to Bill.

Bill and his wife Lyn became good friends. At their place we watched a movie on colour television for the first time. The movie was Swiss Family Robinson and that night we had 220mm of rain!

Eventually, the strike ended. This was a strange moment in Australia's history, and a sad moment. Nobody won, and a lot of people as well as the economy suffered.

The new sheds operated much better than the old ones. Between batches, the feeders and watering system could be winched up out of the way, making cleaning so much easier. At first the winches were operated by hand, using an electric drill. Later, we just had to press a button.

To prepare the sheds, we covered the ground with wood shavings, which the chickens scratched and dug around in. The shavings also soaked up the manure. When a batch went to markets, the old shavings were taken away and new shavings put in.

In the old sheds, old shavings were removed with a shovel and wheelbarrow. In the new sheds, I used a tractor and blade to pile it up for a local dairy farmer and good friend, Bill Young. He picked up the old shavings in his truck and fertilised his farm with it.

By then, with new technology, a batch took 8-10 weeks to fully grow, and we had about three weeks between batches to clean and prepare sheds. Eventually, we found a company that cleaned the sheds and brought fresh bedding material. They charged nothing because they used the old material to feed cattle.

We grew chickens in those sheds for nearly 30 years, and it was a very good investment for us. Building shed 2 meant I could stop working outside the farm and spend more time with my family, also enjoying sport and music.

Challenges with raising chickens

Sudden loud noises frightened the chickens, like drivers beeping their horns or bad lightning and thunder, especially in the night. Terrified chickens stampede and pile up on top of each other, sometimes suffocating many. This was a great concern especially with older chickens, and many times we lost birds this way. I deliberately sang loudly and made loud noises in the sheds to try to prepare them for sudden noises like thunder.

When we had chickens in the old sheds, one night, dogs broke the netting in one shed, and all the chickens got out. When I went down early in the morning, hundreds of dead white chickens were scattered across the ground, killed by the dogs just for the sport. I dug a hole with the tractor to bury them.

One Easter Thursday, we were expecting a full batch to be delivered by truck at 1.30pm. By 4pm, I decided I'd go to look for the late truck. It must have been the busiest road day of the year and with only one lane each way to and from Brisbane, I got as far as Aspley before turning around. Somehow, I missed seeing the delivery truck on the highway because it got to the farm about 15 minutes after I left, and it was nearly 7pm before I got back.

Because the truck had no air conditioning, hundreds of our chickens were dead from the heat. It was a mad rush trying to get the live ones out and on to water.

Another time, we had both big sheds full, with a total of 32,000 chickens. One shed had been emptied, so luckily half of the batch was safe. It was terribly hot weather with only big fans to cool the chickens in the shed. We'd gone to Dohles Rocks to get cool, taking Len and Diana with us. We saw a storm brewing so hurried home to find over 100 of the full-grown chickens dead, most under the fans or piled up on top of each other.

Diana and Len helped us throw out all the dead birds. Another poultry farmer in Narangba, John Twoomey, brought his tractor down to dig a hole and bury them for us. At other times, we helped John and another grower pick up thousands of dead chickens in their sheds, lost during heat waves. Dead birds were thrown straight onto the back of trucks and taken away to a factory, thrown into a machine, and made into canned dog food.

Another unsuccessful batch happened when Len and I were overseas for two months. Apart from an eagle snipping off chicken's heads as they poked through the mesh looking for the sunshine, John Twoomey's and our chickens were put on a trial run using different chicken feed. The chickens did very poorly. Thankfully, we were compensated financially by Ingham's.

In mid-1980's, we had a different challenge with Queensland electricity strikes. Power cuts kept happening and we didn't know how long we'd be without power. The new sheds relied on power 24 hours a day, to power the automatic feeding system and provide lighting during the night. We could lose chickens by the thousands due to starvation if the feed system did not work for a long period. We desperately needed a generator - just when every other business also wanted one. Eventually, we found one, but the price had gone up double because of the strike. We still have that generator in its purpose built shed on the farm.

Changes to the poultry industry and our retirement

Despite the occasional setbacks, growing chickens was a great business for us. From our humble start in 1958, with 100 chickens living in a room in our house, through to growing in a few bush sheds, then new automated sheds carrying 32,000 birds, we saw many changes in the industry.

In the beginning, it took about 15 weeks for chickens to be fully grown. When we retired, that time had reduced to an average of 7-8 weeks and as little as 6 weeks if Ingham's wanted smaller birds. These changes came because of new breeds of chickens, and better foods and facilities.

The changes kept coming because Ingham's wanted to work with larger and more modern operations. They gave us an ultimatum – either double the size of our operation or stop farming. Expanding at Narangba was not permissible due to local planning rules. We looked at buying another farm, but considering our age and the costs involved, we decided to sell our contract with Ingham's to an associate in the industry, Barry Benbow.

This decision was a real blow for us in a way, as not long before, we spent a large amount upgrading our existing sheds. This was money down the drain unfortunately.

Despite that loss, Barry paid us well for the contract, which helped us going into retirement. We retired in 1998, when Betty was 68 and I was 72, and by then, we were one of Ingham's smallest farmers. Now, growers can have 200,000 chickens or more.

FAMILY LIFE

Our life was busy – raising a family, building the farm and chicken business, growing small crops, and working other jobs. Gone were the Italian feste that I loved so much, but we still found time to spend with the children and community.

Our eldest son Tony was a phenomenal student and much of his working life has been in line with his passion to protect and improve the environment.

Both of our daughters, as well as Betty, loved horses and the girls did well competing in gymkhanas and events.

Peter and Len were high standard tennis players, reaching the semi and quarter finals in the State championships for their age groups.

With the boys and me loving the game, we built a tennis court on the farm, originally with compacted dirt from ant beds. Peter had the job of rolling the court with a heavy cement roller to maintain the surface. After a few years, we surfaced the court with flexi-pave. For years I was a member of the local Burpengary fixtures team, and we met many friends through tennis. They often visited the farm for a game and a meal.

These days, the court is old and worn, but still gets plenty of use. Our grandchildren play on it regularly and I use it as a flat surface to safely walk for exercise. Our daughter Diana set up an enormous marquee over the court for her wedding reception. We were so happy when Diana and Len chose to hold their weddings here on the farm.

Apart from tennis, another passion was bowling. Italians love to play bocce, a game like bowls. My grandfather Antonio had a bocce court at his general store and bar in Ari. It wasn't hard to get a game with customers who visited the store, so I played a lot back in Italy.

In about 1960, I joined the Narangba indoor bowls club. Shortly after, I represented our club in the state singles championship. I won the Queensland championship that night. Because of this, I was offered the opportunity to represent Queensland at a state competition in Sydney.

However, due to family and farm responsibilities, plus lack of money and time, it was not possible for me to spend three weeks away at the championships. I wasn't prepared to leave Betty and the kids because Narangba was still a frontier, with no power or town water.

Reuniting with Italian family and friends

In 1988, Len and I travelled to Argentina and then Italy to see our family. It was 36 years since I had set foot in my homeland or seen my family in Italy or Argentina.

Many Australian migrants and refugees will know what it's like to be reunited with family after so long, and here my words fall short. It is not possible to describe my emotions of seeing Natuccia again at her home in Rosario, Argentina.

We hugged and cried and held each other and spent precious time catching up on each other's lives since I emigrated from Italy in 1952 and she in 1953. Franco and Natuccia have two children, Anna and Giovanni, and several grandchildren and great-grandchildren in Rosario. We made a connection with the whole family, which remains a treasure in my heart, even though we have not seen each other again since.

Added to this wonderful reunion, we were also in for a tremendous surprise during this trip. We had the incredible privilege of being invited to dinner at Rosario Italian Club. Here Natuccia and Franco had organised a great surprise.

Practically all the extended family, descendants of my uncles, arrived at the Italian Club that night to meet us and celebrate our visit to Argentina, around 20-30 people in total.
It was one of the most exceptional experiences of my life to meet for the first time a large group of my first cousins and their families. I did not even know that most existed.

By now, the family's language in Argentina had moved from Italian to Spanish, but thankfully there were enough similarities between the languages that we could communicate and share this most memorable night together.

One never forgets times like we had in Argentina, reuniting with family, and meeting new family. My only regret among all the happiness was thinking about how much we all missed by not being together more – the problem of distance when a European makes Australia home.

The generosity of our family during this trip was phenomenal. Natuccia's son-in-law, Alfredo, took us on a sightseeing road trip through central Argentina. From Rosario, we drove north to Iguazu National Park and the famous Cataratas Del Iguaco (Iguazu Falls).

From Argentina, we travelled to Italy, returning to my home village and country. My strong emotion there was the same I had with meeting Natuccia and her family. With great joy, I reunited with my niece Eufemia who was a child when I left in 1952. Eufemia was the only one of Isolina's children who stayed in Italy. Rosalinda had immigrated to Australia, and Rocco spent time in Australia before immigrating to the United States.

It amazes me how family bonds reform and strengthen despite the separation of time and distance. While Eufemia and I stayed in touch over the years, the bond we both felt when we met again was immense. The ties that we reforged with Eufemia, her husband Mario and their two wonderful daughters and their families, remain strong.

Since then, our five children have visited Eufemia and Mario's farm in Vacri and been welcomed by the family. I visited twice more, once to meet up with Len, who was spending time in Europe, and again, years later, in 2010 with Tony.

It brings great joy for me that each of our children (and some grandchildren), have been to the old country, seen where I came from, and connected to the Italian side of our family and history.

During our visit, I reunited with other family members and old friends who live in Vacri, Ari and the neighbouring seaside town of Francavilla al Mare, where I have cousins. Every day of my visit brought back memories and emotions that I will treasure in my heart forever.

Len and I travelled from Vacri through Florence, Venice, Verona, and Milan and had many experiences in between, including a great day in Assisi in Umbria. When I grew up in Italy, never would poor rural farmers think of taking a trip around the country just for pleasure. Of course, I knew of the great cities of Florence, Venice and Milan and their phenomenal artworks, museums and history, but to see these places as a visitor was truly a wonderful and emotional experience for me.

During our travels, we met wonderful locals, always interested in talking and learning about my life and experiences in Australia. In Rome, we discovered the hotel owner knew my father! After we made that connection, he could not do enough for us, providing the best food and accommodation.

In Assisi, we met a Canadian bishop who was having trouble with his bank arrangements. He travelled with us to Rome, with us paying for food and accommodation for him on the way. He paid us back when we got to Rome. Such are the friendships we made while travelling.

Each time I went back to Italy meant the world to me, and I am so grateful to have had these special experiences.

Still singing

I have always loved music, especially traditional Italian folk songs - such a big part of our lives growing up. 'La Campagnola Bella' (The Beautiful Farm Girl) and 'Marina ti Voglio Sposar' (Marina I want to marry you), are still my favourites.

Joining together to play music, sing and dance, brought welcome relief to our impoverished rural lives. If we weren't singing, we'd be whistling. Music lifted our spirits and bonded family and friends together.

On my first trip back to Italy in 1988, passion for the music of my homeland was renewed. I saw again, the role music plays in Italian life, and this had a large effect on me, inspiring me to sing and play music. I came back to Australia carrying a fisarmonica (piano accordion) purchased from my friend, Camillo De Ritis.

My love for music was stirred. Back in Australia, I spent as much time as possible studying music. For 14 years, I learned piano accordion - a challenge with my farming fingers. Betty often played piano accordion with me. Unfortunately, a bad wrist injury cut my accordion playing short. After this, I concentrated on singing traditional Italian folk songs and well-known songs sung by Dean Martin, Frank Sinatra, and Elvis Presley.

Through lessons, I worked hard to find my voice and to sing within a range that suited me. With the help of many people over the years, including our good friend, Rita Feroli, I settled in the baritone range.

In my early 90's, I wrote five of my own songs, first in Italian, then for translation into English. The words and the inspiration behind them are included at the end of my book and I hope you enjoy them.

With help from a family friend, Wesley, I recorded these songs and some of my piano accordion playing on CD, of which I am very proud. Wesley is a true artist who also played accompanying instruments on the CD. I am very grateful to him and his family for their help in producing my album and its artwork.

For me, music and singing are just like exercise! They give life and keep you young! I recommend this to everyone.

Revitalising the farm

About 10 years after my retirement in 2008, our youngest son Len and his wife Renee built a house next door to the farm. Soon after, Len left working in the city to spend more time at the farm and to help Betty and I around the place.

For another 10 years I enjoyed working with Len on the farm, helping with everything from machine work to irrigation. I was fit and healthy all through my 80's and being involved kept me young. Len revitalised the farm, registering it as certified organic and producing lettuce and kale crops.

At the start of this venture, Len and I completed a three-week Permaculture course at Northey Street City Farm in Brisbane. This community garden is covered in edible plants and fruit trees, which is my kind of gardening. Betty loves to grow flowers as well as vegetables, but I've never been interested in growing something you can't eat. For me, the garden is a place to grow, pick, and eat produce as fresh as possible.

I fitted in well in this beautiful food garden and learning at the course. Volunteers and students were from all over the world, and it was a great atmosphere. Everyone had such great passion, and people wanted to learn from others to reinforce their own knowledge and values.

We embraced new ideas and met many interesting people. During or after the courses I was often invited to sing Italian songs. Others played instruments and sang, so it was a great cultural exchange. I was the oldest student ever to complete that Permaculture course!

Crops are still grown here on the farm, although on a smaller scale. One old bush shed still stands. It is home to laying chickens and a few goats. One large chicken shed is converted to a packhouse and the end section to a rustic barn used for weddings and parties. It's funny to think we once grew chickens where brides and grooms now dance at their wedding receptions! The other large shed is converted to a greenhouse, where produce is grown in benches above the ground.

For some years, Len hosted international tour groups, mostly from Japan, and I loved helping students learn about farm life, and singing Italian songs for them.

Still together, still active

Betty and I remain active. We both have gardens, I have my music, and visits from our family are highlights for us. We know that being able to keep living on the farm is a gift from our children. Running and maintaining the property would be impossible without their help.

I am so thankful for this gift because the last thing I wanted was to live in a retirement village or on a small house block. Instead, here on the farm, we have the fresh air and something to get up for every day.

IL FINALE (OF MY BOOK - NOT ME!)

With 94 years of experience, my book could go on for much longer!

I was born into a rural paradise that was turned upside-down by war. Not only did we have to survive the war, but we also had to rebuild from zero after it. Today I would be called an economic refugee, but in those days, fortunately, Australia was inviting people who were willing to work and carve out their own lives to help build a better Australia. I will always be thankful for that opportunity.

For three years, I got a taste of Australian life on the railways, in mines, on cane farms and on Burrinjuck Dam, before meeting Betty in Mount Isa. The rest of my story is with Betty, building the farm and raising five children.

We are proud that each of our children has achieved their goals and made their way in life. Our family, which at the time of writing includes 10 grandchildren and six great-grandchildren, has a unique soul that connects us. Without our family, I could never reflect so positively on what I have achieved. I have also had so many friends join me in the different stages of my journey.

I am also thankful that at 94, I am still physically and mentally active. I exercise every day and remain passionate about my music. I sing every day, starting in the morning, setting a tone of happiness for the day. Even at night, if I have trouble sleeping, I hum a tune to myself, and that helps me to feel content and get back to sleep.

I have recounted my story to the best of my memory. I hope it will encourage others to follow their hearts and to achieve their goals.

Wishing you all happiness, good will, and good music.

Michele

MY SONGS

Morning Star (Stella del Mattino)
During a family function, one of my granddaughters entered looking outstandingly gracious and beautiful for the occasion. The words of this song flowed naturally from the inspiration from this vision, like poetry. These words were later set to music.

MORNING STAR
You are great, beautiful and bright
and the formation of the stars
with moonlight above
will shine on you forever
because you are the star of the stars
you are the morning star
Yes you are great, beautiful and bright
full of finesse
ready to embrace the world
the dream of the mantle of the morning star
brighten the beautiful morning
where exciting dreams enhance profound desire
that only you can offer
and I know that you are a star divine
you are great, beautiful and bright
and the glow of the stars with moonlight above
will shine on you forever
because you are the star of the stars
you are the morning star
This is why we love you so
because you are the star of the stars
this is why we love you so
you are the morning star
the star

STELLA DEL MATTINO

Tu sei cara, tu sei dolce, tu sei brava
Tu sei piena di finezza,
pronto di abbracciare il mondo,
il tuo sogno di bellezza
La stella del mattino emerga
Inluminate il tuo sorriso it tuo cuore e piena di luce
Invigoranto il tuo penziero
La pregiosa stella. Fiorisce dolcemente.
Con il suo vivo ardore.
Verso il tuo sogno di speranza
Tu sei bella, tu sei dolce,
tu sei vivida, tu sei meravigliosa
Tu sei la preziosa stella,
la stella che accente il cuore
la stella del amore, la stella di splendore
splendi giu, splendi giu, splendi giu,tu sei la stella di splendore
splendi giu, splendi giu, splendi giu,
tu sei la stella d'amore
Ecco il dovuto di amare ate
tu sei la stella di splendore ecco il
dovuto di amare
ate tu sei la stella da more

Dream of Love (Il Sogno d'Amore)
One night, after a few drops of my favourite homemade wine, I found myself contemplating the many facets and complexities of love.

DREAM OF LOVE
My love is the foundation
to honour your beautiful vision
my love will challenge your life
my love will challenge your life
It will nurture and connect the rewarding moments
you are my heart, you are my love
you are my heart, you are my love

Love is a startling attraction
to someone who shares a favourite view
to absorb a passionate and creative adventure
you are my heart, you are my love
you are my heart, you are my love

The specialty of love will fulfill all your aspiration
to follow your dream
wherever you are, wherever you are
you'll find your love
When that moment comes you will know
that your heart is happy and fulfilled
Dreaming of your love. Dreaming of your love.

Love is based on dignity, affection,
modesty and destiny
It's so deep it reaches the greatest divine quality
You are my heart, you are my love
You are my heart, you are my love

My love, my love, my love
my love, my love, my love
my love, my love, my love
You are my heart, you are my love

IL SOGNO D'AMORE

La more e sue dolce virtu
crea una visione molto inluminate
momenti belli e deisiderosi
un virtuoso sogno adorante
tiene e sostiene i suoi preziosi volori
dare e avere il gran dono d'amore
la specialita dell-amore espira tanta bellezza
il suo vigoroso affetto culmina i nostri penzieri

La more e il suo grande volore
gode unaffetto piena di gioia
analizando il bene profondo
donando un gran sogno d'amore

I nostri cuori si accentono
credendo al suo dono supremo
verificando il vero amore
quando dice che mi ami
il mio cuore si apre di gioia
son parole di grande dolcezza
animando con grande vigore
tutto il bene del nostro amore

Amore, amore, amore
questo e il dono del nostro amore
Amore, amore, amore
Che contiene il vero amore
Amore, amore, amore
questo e il dono del nostro amore

The Gift of Music (Il Dono Della Musica)
Everyone who performs music well is dedicated to the task. To anyone with artistic ability - keep performing so as not to lose your ability and so you can be all you can be.

THE GIFT OF MUSIC
Music has been always great for me, all my life
When musical events come by, I like to be there
To enjoy the affinity of the music
To admire the immense talent of the performers
Makes a grateful experience for me

The artist's dedication and devotion of music
Ensures their skill will be for everyone
Creating happiness and joy for all
I visualise the gift and contents of the great music
A tower of enormous size
The tower is totally covered with splendid flowers
And from it descend slowly, covering all the valley
And when we go walking we may pick one
Discovering it is an invitation
To join the beauty of the great music
That is a heart warming moment
Music you'll never forget
 Music has been always great
It will be nice and beautiful forever

And if you love the music,
I would love to play it with you
And if you love dancing,
I would love to dance with you
And if you love singing,
I would love to sing with you

O yes we love the music
O yes we love dancing
O yes we love singing
The beautiful song that we love

IL DONO DELLA MUSICA

La musica e sembre gradito
adorante con grande valore
Ascoltanto suonando o cantanto
Il cuore gode di gioia
Gli artisti dedicano i lori tempi preziosi
beneficanto il gran dono supremo
Valutanto con grande dolcezza
gradire e godire tutto il suo bene
che dolcezza, che bellezza
di gradire il suo grande valore
la musica che noi amiamo
Io spero che tempi cosi noi svanira piu
tenento con noi quel valore di dolce vertu
un castello famoso di alta bellezza
manifestava una musica dolce
vivida e meravigliosa
Che dolcezza che bellezza
Fu quel virtuoso momento diserenita
La dolce musica che noi amiamo

E a me piace suonare
E mi piace anche ballare
Ma il mio cuore gode
pure cantare
le dolce canzone che noi amiamo

To Embrace the World (Abbracciare Il mondo)
As a young man migrating to Australia, I embraced this new life and opportunities with great appreciation and enthusiasm. This song was derived from my experiences throughout this journey.

TO EMBRACE THE WORLD
The world is beautiful and admirable
We adore the creation of its beauty
You have to think how illuminating it can be
Invigorating this wonderful world

You open the door in the morning
And you see the lovely sunshine all around
Looking up in the sky
It's brilliance flourishing your journey

The transformation as the hours go by
The beautiful moonlight appears
It looks so impressive
Seeing the decoration of so many stars
The sparkling illumination descends
To brighten this beautiful world

To embracing mountains, crossing rivers
Under the sunshine and moonlight
That we honor and symbolise forever
Embracing this wonderful world

This is the world we live
This is the world we love
It is our beautiful world
The world

ABRACCIANDO IL MONDO

Il mondo e tanto bello e ammirante
noi adoriamo la creazione e le sue bellezze
guardanto con dolcezza impressivo
godento vivmente il suo dono speciale
la trasformazione dopo alcune ore
la luna inluminante appare
circontato e decorato d tante stelle
Il mondo si accente dolcemente
donanto il suo volto adorante
che noi inmenzamente ammiriamo
amare con grande dolcezza

gradire e godire le sue bellezze
abracciando il suo dono speciale
con grante volore
questo e il monolo
del nostro amore
che noi viviamo

abracciando mondi
sorpassando fiumi
sotto il sole e la luna inluminante
abracciando questo mondo amato con gran valore
che noi viviamo

The Sweet Music (La Dolce Musica)
In Roccamontepiano, a small city in the mountains of Italy, I heard the sweet sound of music drifting from a nearby performance. It was such an inspirational moment that this piece was written to celebrate it.

THE SWEET MUSIC
One evening sweet and elegant
was one moment nice and admirable
the place of great value, impressive
creating the nice time animated
the teachers open the special course
everyone ready and attentive
giving to us the sweet melody
the music opens slowly
performing in full serenity
the active event was acclaimed
to the point of extremity
the place serene and attentive
embracing the sweet outcome
describing that moment so adorable
touching every point of its beauty
adoring that panoramic so nostalgic
and it's unique value

LA DOLCE MUSICA

Una sera dolce e elegante
Fu un momento bello e ammirante
Un luogo di valore impressivo
Creanto il bel tempo animato
I maestri aprano il corso speciale
Ognuno di loro pronto e attentivo
Donanto annoi la dolce melodia
La musica previene piano piano
combiento in priena serenita
Lattivo avvenimento fu acclamato
sul punto di estremita
Il luogo cosi sereno e acogliento
Abbracciava il dolce avvenimento
Descrivento quel momento adorante
Toccanto ogni punto di belta
Endrando in que luogo cosi nostalgico
Vedento quel panoramico della sua belta

My grandfather Michelangelo (standing) and my father Giustino. Photo taken in Argentina

My father, Giustino Costantini

My mother's parents, (my grandparents) Antonio Salvatore and Concetta (nee) D'Inzi. Sadly, I have no photograph of my mother

My grandfather Michelangelo (back) and my father Giustino with his first wife Antonietta and their daughter Isolina. Photo taken in Argentina.

My stepmother, Camilla Assunta Ricci

My sister Isolina and husband Luigi Pirozzi

*Engagement photo of my cousins,
Rubano and Elodia Di Luzio, in Italy*

Me about 24 years old

I arrived in Melbourne on the SAN GIORGIO (pictured) in 1952.

***

The SAN GIORGIO made three voyages to Australia in 1952 for the Lloyd Triestino Line. The vessel was built in Italy in 1923 as the "Principessa Giovanna" and traded to Australia until 1925 when she switched to the South American trade. The vessel was substantially rebuilt in the 1930's and saw service during WW2 firstly as an Italian troopship and then as British hospital ship (having been captured in 1944). In 1947 she was again refitted in Genoa and renamed "San Giorgio" and finally scrapped in 1954. Photo & blurb credit: Sydney Heritage Fleet

Bonegilla camp 1954. No known copyright restrictions

Betty and I on our wedding day in 1957

Me at Burrinjuck Dam, trying out a bike that was for sale. Wearing a black sash on my suit lapel in mourning for my father.

Renovating our house at Narangba

Chicken farming

Replacing an old corrugated iron tank on the chicken shed

Cousin Natuccia and her husband Franco

Revisiting the cave which we dug behind the house during the war

Natuccia and me

Picking tomatoes with Eufemia in Vacri

My good friend, Ernie

Me, my brother Antonio, and sister-in-law Giuseppina, in Sydney

With Lucio and Giustino at my 70th birthday

My father's house, where Antonio and I grew up, in Ari

*Me at my father's house where Natuccia and Anna lived.
My father and grandfather were born in this house*

Our community well in Ari, taken over by the Germans in the war

The key to Natuccia and Anna's house

Singing at the Northside Music School.
I had 14 years of piano accordion lessons, followed by 13 years of singing lessons.

An aerial view of our farm

At work on the farm

Playing the piano accordion (fisarmonica) with Betty

Elodia and me

My nephew Rocco, and nieces Rosalinda & Eufemia 2015

Betty and me

My family. Tony, Betty, myself, Linda, Peter, Diana and Len

www.ingramcontent.com/pod-product-compliance
Lightning Source LLC
Chambersburg PA
CBHW061755290426
44109CB00030B/2867